Mythic Voices

ISBN 0-8123-8198-X

Copyright © 1994 by McDougal, Littell & Company
    Box 1667, Evanston, Illinois 60204

Published in 1991 by
Nelson Canada
A Division of Thomson Canada Limited
1120 Birchmount Road
Scarborough, Ontario
M1K 5G4

The editors would particularly like to thank Dana Tenny and Jill Shefrin of the Osborne Collection of Early Children's Books, Toronto Public Library, and the librarians at Boys and Girls House, Toronto Public Library, who gave unstint-ingly of their expertise and time.

Printed and bound in Canada

00 01 02 03 04 05 06 TCP 10 9 8 7 6 5

MYTHIC VOICES

REFLECTIONS IN MYTHOLOGY

CELIA BARKER LOTTRIDGE
ALISON DICKIE

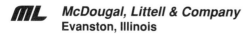

McDougal, Littell & Company
Evanston, Illinois

New York • Dallas • Columbia, SC

CONTENTS

MONSTERS AND MONSTER KILLERS

THE ROMANCE OF THE WARRIOR

ADVENTURES AND WONDER TALES

JOURNEYS TO THE OTHER WORLD

Telling Myth

Before the myths in this book were written down they were told by storytellers, and remembered by listeners who retold them in new places, to new listeners. So the stories grew and changed, borrowing details and events from other stories, as they travelled from one group of people to another, sometimes halfway around the world.

In time the central myths, like most in this book, arrived at a form that did not change very much from telling to telling. The main events and the principal characters were settled, and they were too important to be altered. Still, a storyteller could change words and details to give the myth a special feeling.

When the myths were finally written down (for some this happened thousands of years ago, for some not until the twentieth century) the writers, like the ancient storytellers, found their own individual ways of telling them. The versions selected for this book have been chosen partly because they reflect the oral nature of myth. They are meant to be read aloud. Both the reader and the listeners will get a real sense of the tradition that myth came from.

To get an even stronger sense of the power and meaning of the myths, try telling one yourself. This is not a matter of memorizing words. Read the story you have chosen several times until you know the sequence of events—these are the bones of the myth. Then, like the original myth tellers, bring the bones to life by visualizing the landscape, imagining the action until you can see it all, getting to know the characters. Myths are not realistic stories. Let your imagination go.

When you learn a myth this way, from the inside out, you will find that the words come naturally. Some will come from the written words you started with and some will be your own words.

A telling of myths deserves some attention to atmosphere. The listeners should be seated in a circle or a group. Wait for quiet before you begin. Candles or lamplight add to the ambience. Myths have been remembered and retold because they express things that are important to people. Their telling in our time should reflect the honor that tellers and listeners have given them for so long.

Note: *Everything in boldface type on the following pages was written by the editors.*

CREATION

Who are we? How did we get here? How was the world made? These are the oldest questions in the world. Everyone asks them, and each group of people on the planet has stories of how the earth was formed and how the first people came to be. Some peoples believe a single god made the world and all living things on it. Some think the world has always been; others have stories about a powerful trickster who created the world with the aid of animal helpers. Some groups name a male god as creator; others believe a goddess is the source of life.

The myths recognize the complexity of the universe. Creation is not a one-time event— it is a process. The myths you will read here tell about the very beginning and how the world changed to become the world we know.

Creation myths also symbolize the birth of self-consciousness, and speak of a great human need to know how to live in harmony with each other and with the other creatures on the earth.

The Woman Who Fell from the Sky

COLLECTED BY ELLA ELIZABETH CLARK

The story of the animals who dive in the bottomless waters to bring up a little bit of earth is common in the creation myths of many Native Americans.

In the beginning, there was nothing but water—nothing but a wide, wide sea. The only people in the world were the animals that live in and on water.

Then down from the sky world a woman fell, a divine person. Two loons flying over the water happened to look up and see her falling. Quickly they placed themselves beneath her and joined their bodies to make a cushion for her to rest upon. Thus they saved her from drowning.

While they held her, they cried with a loud voice to the other animals, asking for their help. The cry of the loon can be heard at a great distance over water, and so the other creatures gathered quickly.

As soon as Great Turtle learned the reason for the call, he stepped forth from the council.

"Give her to me," he said to the loons. "Put her on my back. My back is broad."

And so the loons were relieved of their burden. Then the council, discussing what they should do to save the life of the woman, decided that she must have earth to live on. So Great Turtle sent the creatures, one by one, to dive to the bottom of the sea and bring up some earth. Beaver, Muskrat, Diver, and others made the attempt. Some remained below so long that when they rose they were dead. Great Turtle looked at the mouth of each one, but could find no trace of earth. At last Toad dived. After a long time he arose, almost dead from weariness. Searching Toad's mouth, Great Turtle found some earth. This he gave to the woman.

She took the earth and placed it carefully around the edge of Great Turtle's shell. There it became the beginning of dry land. On all sides, the land grew larger and larger, until at last it formed a great country, one where trees and other plants could live and grow. All this country was borne on the back of Great Turtle, and it is yet today. Great Turtle still bears the earth on his back.

After a while, the woman gave birth to twins, who had very different dispositions. Even before they were born, they struggled and disputed. The mother heard one of them say that he was willing to be born in the usual manner; the other angrily refused to be born in that way. So he broke through his mother's side and killed her.

She was buried in the earth, and from her body grew the plants that the new earth needed for the people who were to be created. From her head grew the pumpkin vine, from her breasts the corn, and from her limbs the bean.

The twins were not men, but supernatural beings; they were to prepare the new earth to be the home of man. As they grew up, they showed their different dispositions in everything they did. Finding that they could not live together, each went his own way and took his portion of the earth. Their first act was to create animals of different kinds.

Evil Brother, whose name means "flint-like," created fierce and monstrous animals, to terrify and destroy mankind. He created serpents, panthers, wolves, bears—all of enormous size—and huge mosquitoes that were as large as turkeys. And he made an immense toad that drank up all the fresh water that was on the earth.

Good Brother, at the same time, was creating the harmless and useful animals—the dog, the deer, the moose, the buffalo, and many birds. Among them was the partridge. To the surprise of Good Brother, Partridge rose in the air and flew toward the country of Evil Brother.

"Where are you going?" asked Good Brother.

"I am going to look for water," answered Partridge. "There is none here, and I have heard that there is some in the land of Flint."

Good Brother followed Partridge, and soon he reached the land of

Evil Brother. There he was met by the giant snakes, the fierce beasts, and the enormous insects his brother had created. Good Brother overcame them. He could not destroy them, but he made them smaller and less fierce, so that human beings would be able to master them.

Then Good Brother came to the giant toad. He cut open the toad and let the water flow forth into the land. Thus rivers were formed. Good Brother wanted each stream to have a twofold current, so that one side of the river would flow in one direction and the other side in the opposite direction.

"In this way, people can always float downstream," he explained.

"That would not be good for the people," said Evil Brother. "They should have to work one way."

So he made the rivers flow downstream only. And to make paddling a canoe harder and more dangerous, he created rapids and waterfalls and whirlpools in the rivers.

In a dream, Good Brother was warned by the spirit of his mother to be careful, lest Evil Brother destroy him by treachery. When the twin brothers saw that they would always disagree, they decided to have a duel. The one who was victorious would be the master of the world. They decided also that each of them should tell the other what weapon could destroy him.

"I can be destroyed," said Good Brother, "only if I am beaten to death by a bag full of corn or beans."

"I can be destroyed," said Evil Brother, "only if I am beaten to death with the antler of a deer or the horn of some other animal."

They set off a fighting ground, and Evil Brother started the combat. He struck his brother with a bag of corn or beans, chased him over the fighting ground, and pounded him until he was nearly lifeless. His mother's spirit revived him and he recovered his strength.

Then Good Brother seized a deer's antler, pursued his brother, and beat him until he killed the evil one.

After his death, Evil Brother appeared to his brother and said, "I am going to the far west. Hereafter, all men will go to the west after death."

And so until the Christian missionaries came to our land, the spirits of dead Indians went to the far west and lived there.

Yhi Brings the Earth to Life

BY ERIC AND TESSA HADLEY

This is a creation myth from one of the Aboriginal peoples of Australia. The name of the god "Baiame" is pronounced "By-AH-mee."

There were no stars, no sun, no moon. The earth lay waiting, silent in the darkness. Nothing moved, no wind blew across the barren plain or the bare bones of the mountains. There was neither heat nor cold, alive or dead...nothing...waiting. Who knows how long?

Beyond the earth, Yhi lay waiting too, sleeping the long sleep. It was Baiame the great spirit who broke that sleep.

In the beginning, there was the sound of Baiame whispering across the universe:

"Yhi, awake."

His whisper invaded her dreams.

"Yhi, awake."

Her limbs stirred, her eyelids flickered and opened, and light shone from her eyes flooding across the plain and the mountains.

Yhi stepped down to earth and from that moment, where there had been nothing, there was everything—sound, movement, light.

The earth felt all these things; it woke at that first footstep. At each new step Yhi took it showed what it had dreamed throughout that long dark time. Flowers, trees, shrubs, and grasses sprang up wherever she walked and when she finally stopped to rest the barren plain was lost under a sea of blooms.

As she rested Baiame whispered to her again:

"This is the beginning. The earth has shown you its beauty, but without the dance of life it will not be complete. Take your light into the caves beneath the earth and see what will happen."

The old darkness still ruled under the earth. There were no seeds here to spring into life at her footstep. Instead her light reflected from metallic veins and sparkling opal points in the shadowy rock forms. As she moved the darkness reformed behind her, and voices boomed and echoed:

"No, no, no! Let us sleep, sleep, sleep."

But Yhi never faltered and soon there were new sounds—faint clicks, scrapings, and scratchings which grew louder and louder as the insects crept, flew, and swarmed from every dark corner. Yhi's warmth coaxed them out and she led them up into the plain, into the waiting grass and leaves and flowers where their buzzing and chirruping drowned the dark wailing from below the earth.

This time Yhi did not pause. She strode across the plain while Baiame whispered:

"The ice caves in the mountains—take your light there."

It seemed that Yhi had met her match in the cold blank silence. But somewhere there began the steady drip, drip, drip of water, free at last. Then, a cracking and crashing as great slabs of ice lost their freezing hold on the cave walls. The surface of the ice lakes splintered and new shapes broke through. These shapes flowed and wavered, unlike the dead ice lumps, and fish, snakes, and reptiles were swept out to join the living earth outside as the lakes overflowed.

Yhi pressed on deeper, but this time as she moved from cave to cave it was not solid, resisting ice she met but the touch of fur and feather. Birds and animals gathered to her, and she led them out to add their voices to the new world.

"It is good. My world is alive," Baiame said.

The Making of Gods and People

BY LEON GARFIELD
AND EDWARD BLISHEN

The Greeks had several creation stories. This is the best known one.

I. The War of the Gods and Titans

In the beginning, there was only Gaia, the earth, mother of us all. In the perfect darkness, Uranus the sky raised himself from Gaia, and in darkness he rained down upon her. The rain quickened her and Gaia brought forth life.

The first children of Gaia and Uranus were monsters, the fifty-headed hundred-handed giants. Their aspect was terror, and their father pushed them back again into darkness, into Tartarus, the underworld of blackness beneath the spreading plains and stony mountains of our mother Gaia.

Again there were children, the huge Cyclopes, in human shape but of the size of mountains, with a single staring eye in their cliff-like foreheads. These were forced back into darkness also; and then were the Titans born.

Their name means "Lord," and the Titans were giants, giants in the same form we puny humans have today, giants in the image of the gods that followed them. These ones, at last, Uranus allowed to walk the earth. In the long darkness, Gaia whispered to her children of her anguish, of her elder children forced back into the womb of night. The Titan Cronus, most devious of her children, heard her whispers, and from her he took the adamantine sickle and unmanned his star-speckled father. Drops of blood fell onto the earth. Uranus shrank and drew himself up into the dome of sky, and his son Cronus ruled instead.

Cronus took his sister Rhea, the daughter of earth, for wife, and with her he had children. Yet Cronus feared a child would someday unthrone him, as he had unthroned his father, so as Rhea gave birth to children, he opened wide his mouth and swallowed them. Into his vast belly went divine baby after baby, while great Rhea hid the bitter anger in her heart and planned his overthrow.

Again she bore a son; but this time Rhea hid her baby, and gave Cronus a stone wrapped in swaddling clothes. He swallowed it, and groaning went to sleep, what sleep came to him from the Furies, the spirits of nightmare.

As Cronus slept uneasily, wracked by the Furies, his son grew up from babyhood: immortal Zeus, raised on Mount Ida by the timeless nymphs. When he had reached his power, the god and his Titan mother conspired against the monstrous father, giving him a purgative to drink when he cried out for wine ....

C ronus called for a cupbearer to fetch his honied drink. But his thirst was not quenched. Indeed, it seemed to have been increased by drinking. So a second cup was fetched. He drained it and laughed uneasily. What was thirst after the nights of the Furies? He flung the engraved cup across the room, where it cracked and splintered against the wall. A third cup! The king was still thirsty. "Quickly! Quickly!" He cursed the cupbearer for a creeping fool. Then Rhea, smiling gently, rustled in to calm her lord. Behind her came another cupbearer, with another cup. "Here, Cronus, my lord! Drink! The king must not go thirsty! Drink to your heart's content!"

So Cronus took the cup and drank.

He drank with barely a glance at the strange cupbearer, and the drink was rushing down his throat before an oddness struck him. Though he stood in Rhea's shadow, this cupbearer seemed to shine as if by the light of another, secret sun. And in that same instant he saw a look exchanged between Rhea and the stranger whose shining seemed suddenly menacing. The drink tasted sharp, and his throat began to sting and burn. But it was too late, he had drained the cup. Rhea smiled, and the cupbearer smiled; and Cronus knew that they had poisoned him.

"Who—who are you?" he whispered. The stranger's radiance

seemed to increase till Cronus could not endure to look at him. "Who—are—you?"

"Ask of the Furies, Cronus."

Cronus opened his mouth to scream for help—but no words came. His throat was on fire and needles of pain stabbed at his belly. He fell back as cramps seized him and he began to retch. Wider and wider stretched his gigantic mouth till he felt the tendons split and tear at their roots. There was a tumult in his head—a mighty uproar. The bones of his gaping mouth were cracking and splintering as they were forced apart. And all the while, in his dreadful agony, he saw Rhea, his wife, and Zeus, his son, staring down on him with implacable hate.

Then Cronus began to vomit. Six times the poisoned Titan erupted and, like some shaking mountain, spewed out the fiery inhabitation of his belly. At last it was over; and Cronus stared in dread at what he'd brought forth. They rose up before him like columns of fire; the children he had consumed. In their midst, mockingly cradling the fatal stone with which he'd been deceived, was Rhea. "Behold your sons and daughters!" she shouted. "Behold the avenging gods!" Cronus shrieked and fled.

He fled high up among the granite mountains, stumbling and calling to the universe for help. At last he reached his fortress, and it was there that Atlas and all the Titans of the old order joined him in the war to destroy the gods.

Some say that this war raged for ten years; but there was no certain way of measuring it. Night and day were so obscured that time itself was blinded and could no more than mark the tempests, earthquakes, and scalding storms of the battles. Huge mountains were plucked from the earth and hurled like pebbles against the sky, where they made black holes in the milky fabric of the stars. Again and again the gods approached the fortress of Cronus, and again and again they were beaten back.

In angry despair, Zeus stared up at the mighty stronghold that seemed to have become a part of the very sky. Then he remembered something that the timeless nymphs of Mount Ida had told him—for they were not always singing. They had told him of certain ancient prisoners who still lingered in Tartarus—the Cyclopes and the hundred-handed giants, tremendous children of Mother Earth, who had been forgotten by Cronus in his madness and pride. Even now they raged and rotted in their chains. Even now they waited.

With his brothers Hades and Poseidon, Zeus went down into Tartarus. Through the groves of black poplars and across the wide dark river Styx the three gods moved like flickering flames. Further and further into the dreadful region they voyaged, passing among streaming rocks and between tall cliffs of jet. Now the air grew foul and thick with fog. Briefly the three gods glinted in and among it. Groans and harsh weeping echoed all about them, together with the grinding of chains. Then the air rifted as if worn threadbare by agony and gloom, and through the holes and

The Olympian Gods and the Fates

Zeus divided the rule of the universe with his brothers and sisters. He took the sky and the chief rule, throned on Mount Olympus above the clouds. To Poseidon went the oceans; and Hades descended to the underworld. Their three goddess sisters were given domestic spheres of influence, for this was a patriarchal religion imposed by the warrior Greeks upon the ancient matriarchal religions of the Mediterranean area.

There were twelve great Olympian gods, as well as the gods of the underworld. The Romans had similar gods, and the Roman names are given in parentheses.

First, there were the children of Cronus and Rhea:

1. *Zeus (Jupiter* or *Jove)* was lord of the sky, wielder of the thunderbolt, and father of gods and men. He was a distant ruler, who like all tyrannical fathers insisted on obedience. Most of the Greek heroes and many of the gods are children of Zeus.
2. *Hera (Juno)* was the wife of Zeus, and patron of marriage and childbirth. In Greek mythology she was mostly noted for her terrible jealousy and anger, feelings that reflect the poor condition of women in classical Greece.
3. *Poseidon (Neptune)* was god of the seas, although the seafaring Greeks had such a healthy respect for the dangers of the sea that they continued to invoke earlier sea goddesses and gods as well. He was also the creator of horses and the sender of earthquakes. Since earthquakes can be accompanied by tsunamis (tidal waves), the connection between earthquakes and a sea god is logical.
4. *Demeter (Ceres)* was goddess of vegetation and harvest. The word

rifts the gods saw the gigantic prisoners, chained to the everlasting cliffs. There hung the unbelievable hundred-handed giants, enmeshed in iron; and beside them, so huge that they towered to the height of the cliffs, were chained the Cyclopes, in each of whose single eyes was such pain and despair that even the gods were appalled.

Swiftly the brothers freed them and led them up out of Tartarus. They crossed the river Styx and passed through the groves of black poplars beside the ocean. So vast was the bulk of the creatures who had been freed

---

"cereal" comes from her Roman name. She was one of the most important of the gods, but since she was a goddess of peasants who farmed the earth, she does not appear much in the myths of the warrior aristocracy that ruled Homer's Greece.

5. *Hestia (Vesta)* was the goddess of hearth and home.

The other Olympians were all considered the children of Zeus, although some of them were certainly more ancient than he was:

6. *Hephaestus (Vulcan)*, the first child of Zeus and Hera, was so ugly that at his birth his disgusted mother hurled him out of heaven. The fall made him lame, but he remained devoted to her. He was god of metalworking and fire.

7. *Aphrodite (Venus)* was goddess of love, an aspect of the all-powerful mother goddess whose worship preceded that of Zeus. Beautiful and unpredictable, Aphrodite ruled the hearts of gods and people. She was assisted by *Eros (Cupid)*, personified desire, sometimes called her son.

8. *Ares (Mars)*, another child of Zeus and Hera, was god of war, a swaggering bully hated by his father and virtually everyone else.

9. *Apollo* (also called Apollo by the Romans) was one of the twin children of Zeus and the Titaness Leto. He was one of the most important of the gods, embodying reason, light, prophecy, poetry, and music. He had a dark side too, for he could bring sudden death upon young men.

10. *Artemis (Diana)*, goddess of the moon and young women, was Apollo's twin sister. A virgin, she rejected the company of men. She was also goddess of wild animals, and another aspect of the ancient mother goddess.

that in the darkness the gods seemed like moving stars, followed by a second, blacker night. At last they came to the mountain of Cronus, and the three gods greeted their three sisters who had awaited them. Together the children of Cronus stared at their terrible allies.

The strange eyes of the Cyclopes, set in their heads like monstrous jewels, glinted faintly in the starlight. For the first time since the days of old Uranus they were smiling. They stared up at the fortress in the sky; then they nodded and gave the gods the weapons they would need. To Hades they gave the Helmet of Invisibility, to Poseidon they gave the Trident that shakes the earth, and to mighty Zeus they gave the Thunder-

11. *Hermes (Mercury)*, **child of Zeus and the Titaness Maia, was a complex and fascinating god. Associated with cleverness, communication, creativity, and commerce, he was the messenger of the gods and the mouthpiece of Zeus, as well as the god of thieves. Another duty he had was to guide the souls of the dead to the underworld.**

12. *Athena (Minerva)*, **after whom the city of Athens is named, was one of the most respected of the gods. The myths claim she had no mother: Zeus, the story goes, was overcome by a blinding headache one day, so terrible that he shouted for Hephaestus to bring an axe to split open his head. Athena burst forth from Zeus's head with a shout, to become the ruler of wisdom and war. In her aspect as war goddess, she represented courage and foresight, whereas Ares stood only for bloodlust. Like Artemis, Athena was a virgin, but she was a helper to both men and women. She was accompanied by an owl symbolizing wisdom.**

The gods of the underworld were not considered among the Olympians, although they were ruled by *Hades (Pluto or Dis)*, **the brother of Zeus. After the defeat of Cronus, Hades returned to the upper world only once, to seize the goddess** *Persephone (Proserpine)*, **daughter of Zeus and Demeter, to become his queen in the underworld. Although Hades and Persephone were not spirits of evil, like the devil is for Christians, Jews, and Moslems, the Greeks did fear them and never mentioned their names if they could help it. Rulers of the dead, they also symbolized the fertile power of the earth and all its hidden riches.**

bolt before which all must fall.

Hades put on the helmet. At once he faded so that where the grim god had once stood, was now no more than a shadow such as might have been fancied by a tired eye. Quietly this vague shadow began to drift up the mountain toward the lofty fortress, and the armed gods followed stealthily after.

With the weapons forged by the Cyclopes, and the overwhelming fury of the hundred-handed giants, Zeus overturned the rule of Cronus, and banished the Titans. After that he ruled supreme.

Last of the great gods was *Dionysus (Bacchus)*, a latecomer who was the son of Zeus and a mortal woman. The cult of Dionysus was spread through Greece by women who gained through it a chance to throw off, for a few days, the tedious restrictions of their lives. Dionysus represented wine, communal feeling, and delirious frenzy; mystic insight and powerful inspiration; fertility and life.

In addition to these gods and goddesses, there was a great host of local spirits and powers. Rivers, streams, trees, or any remarkable features of the landscape were likely to have a resident spirit, worshipped by those who lived nearby. These were the nymphs and dryads, fauns and satyrs, and so on.

Although Zeus could rule much as he wished, there was a limit to the things that he could will. There were mysterious older, impersonal powers that even he could not avoid. Such were the Fates.

The Fates, the three sisters who determined the lives of people and the ending of the world, were a common concept in the myths of the European peoples. They represented the power of a primal mother goddess. In Greek myth, they were three blind women at a spinning wheel: Clotho spun the threads of life; Lachesis measured them out; and pitiless Atropos cut them off. The same three figures appear in Norse myth as the Norns, who lived by the Well of Truth at the roots of the World Tree. The Anglo-Saxons knew them as the Wyrds—*Wyrd* is Old English for "Fate." The Fates show up in Shakespeare's *Macbeth* as the three witches—"the weird sisters."

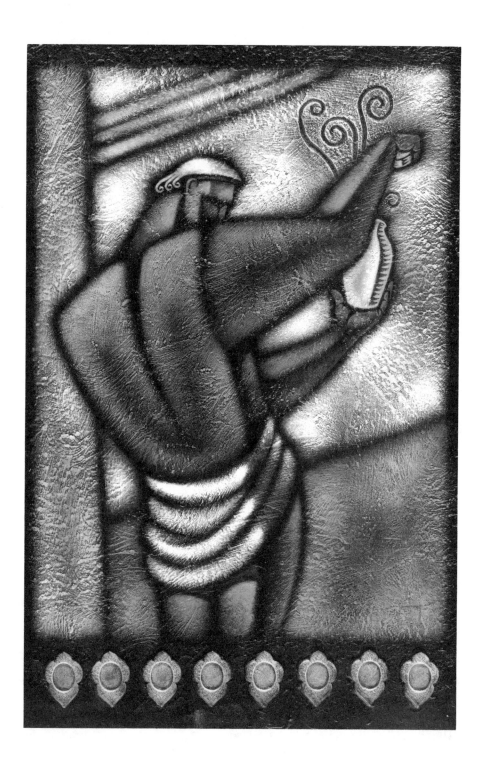

II. The Creatures of Prometheus

Not all the Titans were banished. Giant Atlas, the strong slow-witted friend of Cronus, was compelled to bear the heavens on his shoulders in everlasting punishment. Some Titanesses became the mothers of gods and goddesses. And there was Prometheus.

No figure in Greek myth awakens more echoes in us today than Prometheus. His name means "Forethought," and he was a being of great wisdom and compassion. It was Prometheus the Titan who made us mortal human beings. But he could not protect us from the blind power of the Fates ....

Prometheus had a garden in Attica; a pleasant, cultivated grove in the lap of Mount Hymettus where the wild bees made the honey from which the nymphs distilled the nectar for the gods. Here, the Titan and his brother grew such fruits as the earth would yield, and had built themselves a house round an ancient fig-tree. It had been Hestia herself who had taught them the art of building; and wise Athena had come often to sit and talk of how best to cultivate the soil, while her beloved owl had perched in the wrinkled branches of the tree.

But now the Titans walked among their glades and across their close-cut lawns. Prometheus was troubled; his mighty head was bowed in thought. He feared for the lovely earth.

Little by little the brothers' shadows lengthened as the sun rode down into the sea. Prometheus was silent and Epimetheus, his brother, shrugged his shoulders and returned into the house. Of the two, he was the simpler and did not foresee, as Prometheus did, that present pleasure may be bought too dear.

Prometheus stared through the shadowy leaves of his orchards to the wide expanse beyond.

"All this," he whispered, "to no purpose? It cannot be!"

He raised his unhappy eyes and gazed towards Olympus. He tried to fathom what might be in the mind of almighty Zeus. He did not trust the god. He believed that sooner or later Zeus would beget a child and give it the world to play with. Even a child like murderous Ares. ...

He shivered and knelt down. He took up a handful of the rich earth and crushed it in his fist. He opened his hand. The earth, moist from the rain, had taken the imprint of his fingers. He frowned and tried to mould it further. . . . Angrily he threw it down and strode on to where a stream whispered lazily among tall reeds. Here the soil was heavy with clay and more obedient to the shaping hand. So Prometheus made a second image; and it looked like a little angry Zeus.

Prometheus laughed; then, suddenly, a strange excitement filled him.

He bent down and with both his vast hands gathered up more clay. He scooped out half the bed of the stream, so that the worried waters gushed and gurgled as if in a whirlpool.

Then, when the moon was gone into a cloud and the garden was in darkness, he hastened back to his home with the clay still dripping in his arms. He believed he had been very secret.

There was a room in the Titans' home that belonged to Prometheus alone. Its rafters were formed from the trimmed and polished branches of the fig-tree that still grew from the middle of the floor. It was in this room that Athena had loved to sit and discourse with the profound Titan on matters of the universe, while aloft her owl made two orange suns with its eyes.

The room was rich and heavy with thought. It was here that Prometheus brought the clay and laid it on an oiled and polished bench that stretched for the room's great length.

Under this bench were several stone jars, well stoppered and sealed. No one knew of these jars but the two Titans who had guarded them jealously since the far-off days of murdered Uranus. One of them was cracked and skilfully repaired. The damage had been done during the wild war between the Titans and the gods. A mountain had crashed to blazing ruin and shaken the jar from a shelf. But Prometheus had saved it.

Now at last he broke the seal and opened it. Within was the divine substance of Chaos from which all things had been created.

Prometheus had seen it, still ungrown, lying in a deep pit. It had glimmered and winked up at him. Eagerly he'd gathered it and stored it in the jars.

He poured it out. Everywhere in its shining bulk were the bright, immortal seeds trapped like fireflies in some black, festooning web.

Firmly and quickly the great Titan kneaded this ancient substance into the riverbed clay, till the precious seeds were evenly distributed. Then he set to work in earnest.

Prometheus shaped the clay into images of the immortal gods. His fingers grew more and more skilful as his great mind wrestled with the mysterious quest for form. His memory and imagination seemed to body forth shapes in the air, and swiftly he enclosed them in the curious clay.

Little Zeuses, Heras, Apollos and Poseidons ran from his fingertips; even a dark-browed Hades and a proud Artemis with a wart on her knee where the Titan's finger had fumbled.

Then he set the little godkins up before him and rested his mighty head on his aching hands. Already the immortal seeds had begun to stir and grow within the thick, insensitive clay. Quietly, the Titan watched.

But he was not the only watcher. High among the crooked rafters perched an intent bird. It was a crane whose bright, bright eyes were the eyes of Hermes. . . .

The clay was swelling, growing. Channels were being formed within it, down which the burst seeds sent crimson tears to course, nourishing, coloring, and warming into life.

Eyelids grew thin as gauze, flicked open to reveal strange little pools of wonderment. Lips reddened, parted on white teeth . . . and tongues began to stir under the force of mounting breath.

And still they grew till their proportions were all but godlike. Everywhere in the vast room limbs were stretching, bodies twisting, and hair stirring in the night breeze.

At last, they grew no more. The seeds had spent themselves; their task was done. The great Titan smiled.

"Go," he whispered. "Go seek your inheritance before it is too late."

His door was open, and the starlight drifting in glinted on their sweet new limbs.

They turned their faces back to the vast dark room in which they had been made. Their eyes met the deep eyes of Prometheus. They smiled— and then they went out into the glorious garden of the night.

The Titan watched them, and inexplicably his eyes grew full of tears and his huge heart ached with love and hope for the creatures he had made.

Suddenly one gave a wild, wild cry and fell at the foot of a poplar tree. Prometheus hastened to his side; stared down, touched—then recoiled. His new-made child was cold and still.

In the groin of the gaunt mountain of the Fates, the three blind, stonefaced creatures laughed. Atropos fingered her shears. The blades were sharp. To test them—just to test them—she had slit a new-spun thread.

Prometheus knelt beside his cold, quiet creation, not instantly knowing what was amiss, what had fled.

The watchful crane that had perched on the rafters was gone. Hermes the messenger had taken a shade to the echoing world of the dead. Alone and bewildered, it flitted on the further bank of the River Styx.

The first man had died.

"So frail a thread?" whispered Prometheus. "Was it the clay…or the seeds themselves? I had hoped—but it was not to be. What can you do against the gods and the Fates with the fragile, pitiful life I've given you?"

Then Prometheus buried his dead in the shadow of the poplar tree and mourned till it was light.

Hermes brought word to Zeus, and Zeus swore that if these pitiful creatures of Prometheus lived, they would live as animals, not knowing fire, forbidden all knowledge that might let them approach the power of the gods.

In defiance of great Zeus, in dark, at night, Prometheus ventured up the steep side of Mount Olympus, to the forge of the smith god Hephaestus. There, at the fiery furnace, he kindled a spark of the divine fire and took it down the mountain inside a hollow stalk of fennel. At dawn, here and there across the broad face of the earth a wispy trail of smoke straggled up to heaven, and by these signs Zeus knew his order was denied.

Along with fire, Prometheus gave his children all useful arts: he taught them how to till the earth and tame the animals; how to build homes for shelter, and to mine metals from the ground and forge them into tools; and knowledge of healing of the body and the mind.

Zeus watched all this, meditating his fury at the Titan's disobedience, at last sending his iron guards Force and Might to seize Prometheus. They took him to the bleak crags of distant ice-shrouded mountains, to nail him to the rock in chains that could not be broken. There Zeus set no limit on his punishment and sent redoubled agony upon him: a loathsome vulture each day ripped up his tender belly to eat the liver, and each chill night the liver grew back afresh for the next day's torment. There Prometheus endured in agony the fury of a tyrant god whose rule was blind obedience.

Yet Prometheus knew that he had seen two tyrants fall, and he awaited the ending of the third, who now reigned on Olympus. On his distant mountain, bound in suffering, the Titan awaited one who would deliver him.

Pandora's Box

Although Prometheus was punished for his disobedience, Zeus was afraid that the powers the Titan had given to his creatures would allow them to equal the gods. The Greek poet Hesiod tells the story of how Zeus decided to prevent this, by commanding Hephaestus to create Woman. The gods called her *Pandora*, "All-giving," and she was a creature of ravishing beauty. She was given as a wife to Epimetheus, the not-so-clever brother of Prometheus, who found Pandora so beautiful he forgot his brother's advice, which was not to take any gift from Zeus.

Zeus sent a wedding present with Pandora—a bronze jar, which he told her never to open. He knew that she would be unable to resist doing what she had been told not to do. That was the way she had been made, after all. One day Pandora felt bored, so she opened the jar to see what was so very secret. Out flew a stinging cloud of horrid shapes—all the diseases, miseries, and evils that plague our lives today. They had been created by Zeus as his curse upon humanity. The last thing in the jar was hope, the only thing that makes our lives bearable.

The Raven Steals the Light

BY BILL REID AND
ROBERT BRINGHURST

In this story, it isn't fire that is stolen, but light itself.

a long time ago

Before there was anything, before the great flood had covered the earth and receded, before the animals walked the earth or the trees covered the land or the birds flew between the trees, even before the fish and the whales and seals swam in the sea, an old man lived in a house on the bank of a river with his only child, a daughter. Whether she was as beautiful as hemlock fronds against the spring sky at sunrise or as ugly as a sea slug doesn't really matter very much to this story, which takes place mainly in the dark.

Because at that time the whole world was dark. Inky, pitchy, all-consuming dark, blacker than a thousand stormy winter midnights, blacker than anything anywhere has been since.

The reason for all this blackness has to do with the old man in the house by the river, who had a box which contained a box which contained a box which contained an infinite number of boxes which nestled in a box slightly larger than itself until finally there was a box so small all it could contain was all the light in the universe.

The Raven, who of course existed at that time, because he had always existed and always would, was somewhat less than satisfied with this state of affairs, since it led to an awful lot of blundering around and bumping into things. It slowed him down a good deal in his pursuit of food and other fleshly pleasures, and in his constant effort to interfere and to change things.

Eventually, his bumbling around in the dark took him close to the home of the old man. He first heard a little singsong voice muttering away. When he followed the voice, he soon came to the wall of the house, and there, placing his ear against the planking, he could just make out the words, "I have a box and inside the box is another box and inside it are many more boxes, and in the smallest box of all is all the light in the world, and it is all mine and I'll never give any of it to anyone, not even to my daughter, because, who knows, she may be as homely as a sea slug, and neither she nor I would like to know that."

It took only an instant for the Raven to decide to steal the light for himself, but it took a lot longer for him to invent a way to do so.

First he had to find a door into the house. But no matter how many times he circled it or how carefully he felt the planking, it remained a smooth, unbroken barrier. Sometimes he heard either the old man or his daughter leave the house to get water or for some other reason, but they always departed from the side of the house opposite to him, and when he ran around to the other side the wall seemed as unbroken as ever.

Finally, the Raven retired a little way upstream and thought and thought about how he could enter the house. As he did so, he began to think more and more of the young girl who lived there, and thinking of her began to stir more than just the Raven's imagination.

"It's probable that she's as homely as a sea slug," he said to himself, "but on the other hand, she may be as beautiful as the fronds of the hemlock would be against a bright spring sunrise, if only there were light enough to make one." And in that idle speculation, he found the solution to his problem.

He waited until the young woman, whose footsteps he could distinguish by now from those of her father, came to the river to gather water. Then he changed himself into a single hemlock needle, dropped himself into the river and floated down just in time to be caught in the basket which the girl was dipping in the river.

Even in his much diminished form, the Raven was able to make at least a very small magic—enough to make the girl so thirsty she took a deep drink from the basket, and in doing so, swallowed the needle.

The Raven slithered down deep into her warm insides and found a soft, comfortable spot, where he transformed himself once more, this time into a very small human being, and went to sleep for a long while. And as he slept he grew.

The young girl didn't have any idea what was happening to her, and of course she didn't tell her father, who noticed nothing unusual because it was so dark—until suddenly he became very aware indeed of a new presence in the house, as the Raven at last emerged triumphantly in the shape of a human boychild.

He was—or would have been, if anyone could have seen him—a strange-looking boy, with a long, beak-like nose and a few feathers here and there. In addition, he had the shining eyes of the Raven, which would have given his face a bright, inquisitive appearance—if anyone could have seen these features then.

And he was noisy. He had a cry that contained all the noises of a spoiled child and an angry raven—yet he could sometimes speak as softly as the wind in the hemlock boughs, with an echo of that beautiful other sound, like an organic bell, which is also part of every raven's speech.

At times like that his grandfather grew to love this strange new member of his household and spent many hours playing with him, making him toys and inventing games for him.

As he gained more and more of the affection and confidence of the old man, the Raven felt more intently around the house, trying to find where the light was hidden. After much exploration, he was convinced it was kept in the big box which stood in the corner of the house. One day he cautiously lifted the lid, but of course could see nothing, and all he could feel was another box. His grandfather, however, heard his precious treasure chest being disturbed, and he dealt very harshly with the would-be thief, threatening dire punishment if the Ravenchild ever touched the box again.

This triggered a tidal wave of noisy protests, followed by tender importuning, in which the Raven never mentioned the light, but only pleaded for the largest box. That box, said the Ravenchild, was the one thing he needed to make him completely happy.

As most if not all grandfathers have done since the beginning, the old man finally yielded and gave his grandchild the outermost box. This contented the boy for a short time—but as most if not all grandchildren have done since the beginning, the Raven soon demanded the next box.

It took many days and much cajoling, carefully balanced with well-planned tantrums, but one by one the boxes were removed. When only a few were left, a strange radiance, never before seen, began to infuse the darkness of the house, disclosing vague shapes and their shadows, still too dim to have definite form. The Ravenchild then begged in his most pitiful voice to be allowed to hold the light for just a moment.

His request was instantly refused, but of course in time his grandfather yielded. The old man lifted the light, in the form of a beautiful incandescent ball, from the final box and tossed it to his grandson.

He had only a glimpse of the child on whom he had lavished such love and affection, for even as the light was traveling toward him, the child changed from his human form to a huge, shining black shadow, wings spread and beak open, waiting. The Raven snapped up the light in his jaws, thrust his great wings downward and shot through the smokehole of the house into the huge darkness of the world.

That world was at once transformed. Mountains and valleys were starkly silhouetted, the river sparkled with broken reflections, and everywhere life began to stir. And from far away, another great winged shape launched itself into the air, as light struck the eyes of the Eagle for the first time and showed him his target.

The Raven flew on, rejoicing in his wonderful new possession, admiring the effect it had on the world below, reveling in the experience of being able to see where he was going, instead of flying blind and hoping for the best. He was having such a good time that he never saw the Eagle until the Eagle was almost upon him. In a panic he swerved to escape the savage outstretched claws, and in doing so he dropped a good half of the light he was carrying. It fell to the rocky ground below and there broke into pieces—one large piece and too many small ones to count. They bounced back into the sky and remain there even today as the moon and the stars that glorify the night.

The Eagle pursued the Raven beyond the rim of the world, and there, exhausted by the long chase, the Raven finally let go of his last piece of light. Out beyond the rim of the world, it floated gently on the clouds and started up over the mountains lying to the east.

Its first rays caught the smokehole of the house by the river, where the old man sat weeping bitterly over the loss of his precious light and the treachery of his grandchild. But as the light reached in, he looked up and for the first time saw his daughter, who had been quietly sitting during all this time, completely bewildered by the rush of events.

The old man saw that she was as beautiful as the fronds of a hemlock against a spring sky at sunrise, and he began to feel a little better.

The Archer and the Moon Goddess

BY SHIU L. KONG AND
ELIZABETH K. WONG

These stories explain how the sun and moon became the way they are today.

I. The Downing of the Nine Suns

When the world began, Dijun the Sun God and his wife had ten sons. These sons were winged birds of fire and served as suns in the sky.

Dijun worked out a schedule so that only one of his sons would be perched on the Fusong Tree each day, giving off just the right amount of heat and light to the earth. When it was not their turn, the nine other sons rested in the sea.

One day, having had enough of the monotony of sitting alone in the tree all the time, the ten sons rebeled against their parents and flew up into the tree together. This brought disaster to the earth, as the combined rays of the ten suns seared and scorched its surface.

The heat and light were so intense that the earth's inhabitants had to hide in deep, dark holes. Even the rocks and metals were slowly melting away. Nothing could escape the burning rays.

The people of earth prayed to the gods for help. The Sun God and Goddess tried to persuade their children to stop their nonsense, but to no avail.

However, there was a god by the name of Yi who was very concerned about the plight of the people. He asked Dijun if he might have permission to shoot the rebels down.

At first, Dijun was extremely reluctant to allow his sons to be treated in this way. However, when nothing else worked, he finally consented. He gave Yi a magic bow and a quiver of red arrows. "Do what you must," he told Yi, "but please do not hurt my children any more than is necessary."

Yi was the best archer of the universe. He was also a compassionate god, and proposed shooting down the sun birds only because it was the last resort to stop the suffering on earth.

Yi went down to earth and climbed the highest mountain. He showed the sunbirds his magic bow, but they ignored his warning as they had ignored all the others.

Left with no alternative, Yi fitted an arrow to his bow. He took aim and let the bolt fly.

An instant later, a ball of fire hurtled down to the ground. The sunlight was dimmed slightly, and the heat was less overwhelming. When people went to examine the fallen bird, they saw a huge, three-footed raven lying in a crumpled heap on the ground.

Yi shot down two more suns before he paused. Even though three of their brothers had been rendered useless, the other firebirds refused to give up.

Yi was angered by their stubbornness, and fired arrow after arrow at the dazzling sources of light in the sky.

When his fury had subsided, the people on earth counted nine dead ravens on the ground. Yi had one more arrow in his quiver. If he had used all ten arrows, the people realized, there would have been no suns left, and no more light or warmth. What a close call that had been.

The last sun left in the sky learned his lesson from this unnerving event. From then on he never disobeyed his parents.

II. Chang O's Flight to the Moon

After shooting down the nine suns and thus saving earth's inhabitants from death, the Great Archer Yi returned to heaven. He found that Dijun was very angry with him, even though Dijun himself had given the order for his sons to be punished.

"Why did you shoot down nine of our sons all at once?" he asked Yi, in a rage. "How could you inflict such a great loss on myself and my wife? If you love earth and its people so much, you and your wife must go to live

there. I cannot bear to have you in my sight. Your presence will always remind me of my grief for my boys."

Thus Yi and his wife, Chang O, were banished from heaven.

Even though humans loved Yi very much and admired his beautiful wife, the immortal couple did not find it easy to adjust to life on earth. Chang O, especially, was unhappy.

"What have I done to deserve this?" she complained bitterly to her husband. "Why should I, a goddess by birth and brought up in heavenly comfort, be blamed for your misdeeds?"

As time went on, she continued to complain and bemoan the fate that had coupled her with a disgraced god. The domestic difficulties with his wife added to Yi's disappointment at being exiled for his successful and benevolent mission.

But he worked hard to establish as normal a life as possible on earth. He roamed the mountain forests all day, searching for game. He helped people to defend themselves against the attacks of wild beasts and monsters. Gradually, he began to adapt himself to his new life. But, however much he tried to make their life comfortable, his wife refused to become accustomed to living on earth. In fact, she never stopped reproaching him.

"To think that we gods should have to become mortal like humans and, one day, to die like them," she lamented. "I cannot bear the thought of going down to the underworld and being in the company of those terrible ghosts. Oh, if only you had not shot down the nine suns!"

Though the Great Archer had no regrets for what he had done to help the suffering of the people, he tried to work out a way that would spare his wife and himself the horrible fate of living in hell. Chang O realized her husband's concern.

One day, she said to Yi in a softer voice, "My dear husband, I was told that the Queen Mother of the West, who lives in the magnificent Jade Palace on the highest peak of the Kunlun Mountains, has a special magical elixir. Would you go and see if you can charm her into giving us enough potion to render us immortal? Though we are no longer gods, this wretched human existence is at least better than becoming gruesome ghosts in hell."

"I will get the elixir for you, my dear wife, no matter how difficult it may be," Yi promised.

The Kunlun Mountains, the legendary home of the Chinese race, are located to the west of China. The mountain where the Jade Palace was situated was surrounded by a moat filled with "weak water," upon which even the lightest bird feather could not float. This moat was encircled by a desert so hot and barren that flames burned in it, day and night. It was known that no mortal could cross these two barriers alive.

The Queen Mother of the West was reputed to be a monster. She was thought to have the face of a woman, the body of a beast, and the tail of a leopard. Her palace was guarded by giant three-headed bluebirds that hovered in the sky above the palace. Any intruder that was sighted would be pecked to death.

By sheer determination, aided by some supernatural power he still possessed, Yi managed to reach the impenetrable Jade Palace. The Queen Mother granted him audience in her magnificent jade hall. Yi related his unhappy story, and asked the Queen Mother to have mercy on himself and his wife by giving them some of her elixir so that they could escape the miseries of hell. The goddess was moved by Yi's courage and his unfair treatment by the Sun God. She went to her chamber and returned with a small bottle. Handing it to Yi, she said, "This is the Elixir of Immortality. If you and your wife each share half of it, you will live forever on earth. However, if one of you were to drink all of it at once, he or she would become a god again in heaven.

"Guard this potion well, for it is the essence of a magic peach tree. This tree flowers only once every three thousand years. Its fruit takes another three thousand years to ripen. Even then, the harvest is scanty. All the elixir I have is here in this bottle. Take it, and use it wisely."

Yi was greatly touched by the Queen Mother's extreme generosity. With tears streaming down his cheeks, he did not utter a word but slowly knelt before his benefactor in gratitude.

Chang O was jubilant when she saw that Yi had returned with the bottle of elixir. She was even more elated when he told her that a person could actually attain godly status by drinking the entire contents of the bottle. She immediately contrived a secret plan.

The next morning, Yi rose early to go hunting. Before he left, he told Chang O to guard the elixir very carefully. He said cheerfully, "My dear wife, I will hunt enough food for a feast tonight. This elixir warrants a special celebration. After dinner we shall share this precious potion, and then we shall be able to live together forever on this beautiful planet, earth."

Chang O anxiously watched her husband through the window when he left for the hills. As soon as he disappeared into the distance, she took hold of the little bottle. Then she paused for a moment. Did she really want to forsake Yi forever on earth? She knew that if she drank the entire potion, she would probably never see her husband again. But after a few moments' thought she decided to return to her former godly self. Since Yi loved earth so much, she reasoned, he would be able to find happiness even without her. With this thought in mind, she emptied the entire contents of the bottle into her mouth.

The magic potion took effect instantly. Chang O felt her body gradually drifting upwards, pulled by a celestial force. She had not realized that the potion would work so suddenly, and was taken by surprise. She thought with regret of her husband, to whom she had not had a chance to say goodbye.

Since no one was around to help her, she quickly found herself levitated to a great altitude. Around her, the stars were shining and the moon was not far away.

The farther she drifted away from earth, the more remorse Chang O felt for her selfishness. She began to realize that a great many of her friends both in heaven and on earth might not forgive her for leaving Yi behind. So she decided to land on the moon instead of going back to her old home in heaven.

But the moon is far from being the romantic place that people imagine it to be. The terrain was desolate and grey, and the air was freezing cold. Except for a single cassia tree and a small rabbit, there was no other sign of life on the moon. Disillusioned, Chang O began to realize the full consequence of her selfishness. It had caused her to forsake an immortal life with a loving husband for an immortal life of infinite loneliness.

Sedna, Mother of the Sea Animals

BY RONALD MELZACK

Perhaps the best known of all Inuit myths, this is about the creation of the animals on whom the Inuit depended for life.

Long ago, there were no seals or walruses for the Inuit to hunt. There were reindeer and birds, bears and wolves, but there were no animals in the sea. There was, at that time, an Inuit girl called Sedna who lived with her father in an igloo by the seashore. Sedna was beautiful, and she was courted by men from her own village and by others who came from faraway lands. But none of these men pleased her and she refused to marry.

One day, a handsome young hunter from a strange far-off country paddled his kayak across the shining sea toward the shores of Sedna's home. He wore beautiful clothes and carried an ivory spear.

He paused at the shore's edge, and called to Sedna, "Come with me! Come to the land of the birds where there is never hunger and where my tent is made of the most beautiful skins. You will rest on soft bear skins, your lamp will always be filled with oil, and you will always have meat."

Sedna at first refused. Again he told her of the home in which they would live, the rich furs and ivory necklaces that he would give her. Sedna could no longer resist. She left her father's home and joined the young hunter.

When they were out at sea, the young man dropped his paddle into the water. Sedna stared with fright as he raised his hands toward the sky, and, before her eyes, they were transformed into huge wings—the wings of a Loon. He was no man at all, but a spirit bird, with the power to become a human being.

Sedna sat on the Loon's back and they flew toward his home. When they landed on an island in the sea, Sedna discovered that the Loon had lied to her. Her new home was cold and windy, and she had to eat fish brought to her by the Loon and by the other birds that shared their island.

Soon she was lonesome and afraid, and she cried sadly, "Oh father, if you knew how sad I am, you would come to me and carry me away in your kayak. I am a stranger here. I am cold and miserable. Please come, and take me back."

When a year had passed and the sea was calm, Sedna's father set out to visit her in her far-off land. She greeted him joyfully and begged him to take her back. He lifted her into his boat, and raced across the sea toward home.

When the Loon spirit returned, he found his wife gone. The other birds on the island told him that she had fled with her father. He immediately took the shape of a man, and followed in his kayak. When Sedna's father saw him coming, he covered his daughter with the furs he kept in his boat.

Swiftly the Loon spirit rushed alongside in his kayak.

"Let me see my wife," he cried.

Sedna's father refused.

"Sedna," he called out, "come back with me! No man could love you as much as I do."

But Sedna's kayak flashed across the water. The Loon man stopped paddling. Sadly, slowly, he raised his hands towards the sky and once again they became wings. He flew over the kayak that was carrying his Sedna away from him. He hovered over the boat, crying the strange, sad call of the Loon. Then he plunged down into the sea.

The moment the Loon spirit disappeared, the sea waves began to swell up in fury. The sea gods were angry that Sedna had betrayed her husband. The kayak rose and fell as huge waves lashed against it. Sedna's father was terrified, and to save himself he pushed Sedna overboard. Sedna rose to the surface and her fingers gripped the edge of the kayak. But her father, frenzied with fear that he would be killed by the vengeful sea spirits, pulled out a knife and stabbed her hands.

Then, it is said, an astonishing thing happened, perhaps because the Loon spirit or the sea spirits had willed it: the blood that flowed from Sedna's hands congealed in the water, taking different shapes, until suddenly two seals emerged from it. Sedna fell back into the sea, and coming back again, gripped the boat even more tightly. Again her father stabbed her hands and the blood flowed, and this time walruses emerged from the blood-red sea. In desperate fear for his life, he stabbed her hands a third time, and the blood flowed through the water, congealed, and the whales grew out of it.

At last the storm ended. Sedna sank to the bottom of the sea, and all the sea animals that were born from her blood followed her.

Sedna's father, exhausted and bitter, at last arrived home. He entered his igloo and fell into a deep sleep. Outside, Sedna's dog, who had been her friend since childhood, howled as the wind blew across the land.

That night, Sedna commanded the creatures of the sea that had emerged from her blood to bring her father and her dog to her. The sea animals swam furiously in front of her father's igloo. The tides ran higher and higher. They washed up the beach until they demolished the igloo and carried Sedna's father and her dog down to the depths of the sea. There they joined Sedna, and all three have lived ever since in the land of the waters.

To this day, Eskimo hunters pray to Sedna, goddess of the seas, who commands all the sea animals. She is vengeful and bitter, and men beg her to release the animals that were born of her so that they may eat. By her whim, a man successfully harpoons seals and walruses or is swept away from land by the stormy seas. The spirits of the great medicine men swim down to her home and comb her hair, because her hands still hurt. And if they comb her hair well, she releases a seal, a walrus, or a whale.

How the Rivers First Came on Earth

COLLECTED BY
HAROLD COURLANDER

A myth about the first people to live on earth.

In the very, very, very ancient time, an old man named Etim 'Ne (Old Person) came down from the sky, he alone with his old wife Ejaw (Wildcat). At that time there were no people on the earth. This old couple were the very first to go down to dwell there.

Now up to this time all water was kept in the kingdom of Obassi Osaw. On earth there was not a single drop.

Etim 'Ne and his wife stayed for seven days, and during that time they had only the juice of plaintain stems to drink or cook with.

At the end of that time the old man said to his old wife: "I will go back to Obassi Osaw's town and ask him to give us a little water."

When he arrived at the old town where they used to dwell, he went to the house of Obassi and said: "Since we went down to earth we have had no water, only the juice which we sucked from the plaintain stems. For three nights I will sleep in your town, then when I return to earth I hope that you will give me some water to take with me. Should my wife have children they will be glad for the water, and what they offer to you in thanksgiving I myself will bring up to your town."

On the third morning, very early, Obassi Osaw put the water charm in a calabash, and bound it firmly with tie-tie. Then he gave it to Etim 'Ne, and said: "When you wish to loose this, let no one be present. Open it, and you will find seven good gifts inside. Wherever you want water, take out one of these and throw it on the ground."

Etim 'Ne thanked Lord Obassi, and set out on his way earthward. Just before he came to the place where he had begun to cut farm, he opened the calabash, and found within seven stones, clear as water. He made a small hole and laid one of the stones within it. Soon a little stream began to well out, then more and more, till it became a broad lake, great as from here to Ako.

Etim 'Ne went on and told his wife. They both rejoiced greatly, but he thought: "How is this? Can a man be truly happy, yet have no child?"

After two days his wife came to him and said: "Obassi is sending us yet another gift. Soon we shall be no longer alone on earth, you and I."

When the due months were passed, she bore him seven children, all at one time. They were all sons. Later she became pregnant again, and this time bore seven daughters. After that she was tired, and never bore any more children.

In the course of time the girls were all sent to the fatting-house. While they were there Etim 'Ne pointed out to his seven sons where he would like them to build their compounds. When these were finished, he gave a daughter to each son and said: "Do not care that she is your sister. Just marry her. There is no one else who can become your wife."

The eldest son dwelt by the first water which Etim 'Ne had made, but to each of the others he gave a lake or river—seven in all.

After one year, all the girls became pregnant. Each of them had seven children, three girls and four boys. Etim 'Ne said: "It is good." He was very happy. As the children grew up he sent them to other places.

Now the seven sons were all hunters. Three of them were good, and brought some of their kill to give to their father, but four were very bad, and hid all the meat, so that they might keep everything for themselves.

When Etim 'Ne saw this, he left the rivers near the farms of his three good sons, but took them away from the four bad boys. These latter were very sad when they found their water gone, so they consulted together and said: "We are seven, your children. First you gave the water to all. Now you have taken it away from us four. What have we done?"

Etim 'Ne answered: "Of all the meat you killed in the bush you have brought none to me. Therefore I took away your rivers. Because you have come to beg me I will forgive you, and will give you four good streams. As your children grow and multiply I will give you many."

After another year the sons had children again. When the latter grew up they went to different places and built their houses.

When these were ready, Etim 'Ne sent for all the children and said: "At dawn tomorrow, let each of you go down to the stream which flows by the farm of his father. Seek in its bed till you find seven smooth stones. Some must be small and some big like the palm of your hand. Let each of you go in a different direction, and after walking for a while, lay a stone upon the ground. Then walk on again and do the same, till all are finished. Where you set a big stone a river will come, and where you set a small stone a stream will come."

All the sons did as they were bidden, save one alone. He took a great basket and filled it with stones. Then he went to a place in the bush near his own farm. He thought: "Our father told us, if you throw a big stone a river will come. If I throw down all my stones together, so great a water will come that it will surpass the waters of all my brothers." Then he emptied his basket of stones all in one place, and behold! Water flowed from every side, so that all his farm, and all the land round about became covered with water. When he saw that it would not stop but threatened to overflow the whole earth he grew very much afraid. He saw his wife running, and called to her: "Let us go to my father." Then they both ran as hard as they could towards the house of Etim 'Ne.

Before they reached it the other children, who had been setting the smooth stones in the bush, as their father had told them, heard the sound of the coming of the waters. Great fear fell upon them, and they also dropped what remained and ran back to Etim 'Ne.

He also had heard the rushing of the water and knew what the bad son had done. He took the magic calabash in his hand and ran with his wife to a hill behind their farm. On this there grew many tall palm trees. Beneath the tallest of these he stood, while his children gathered round one after the other as they got back from the bush. Etim 'Ne held on high the calabash which Obassi had given him, and prayed: "Lord Obassi, let not the good thing which you gave for our joy turn to our hurt."

As he prayed the water began to go down. It sought around till it found places where there had been no water. At each of these it made a bed for itself, great or small, some for broad rivers, and some for little streams. Only where the bad son had emptied his basket it did not go back, but remained in a great lake covering all his farm, so that he was very hungry, and had to beg from his brothers till the time came for the fruits to ripen in the new farm which he had to cut.

After many days Etim 'Ne called all his children around, and told them the names of all the rivers and of every little stream. Then he said, "Let no one forget to remember me when I shall have left you, for I it was who gave water to all the earth, so that everyone shall be glad."

Two days afterwards he died. In the beginning there were no people on the earth and no water. Etim 'Ne it was who first came down to dwell with his old wife Ejaw, and he it was who begged water from Obassi Osaw.

Nanabush Creates the World

COLLECTED BY EMERSON
AND DAVID COATSWORTH

Stories about Nanabush—also called Nanabozho, Manabozo, and many other variants—are endless, and they are still being told today. Like Raven, Nanabush is a powerful creator and savior of the people.

In the beginning, so the Ojibwa story tellers say, the world in which we live did not exist. In its place was a far older world, the home of the first birds and animals, and of the mighty magician, Nanabush.

To look at Nanabush, you would have thought him quite an ordinary sort of man. Unless you had seen him performing his deeds of wonder, you would never have imagined that it was he, and he alone, who created the world we see around us today. So powerful a magician was he, that he could turn himself into an animal, an old tree stump, or a maple leaf—simply by wishing it!

Now in the old world, which existed long before our world, Nanabush and his young brother lived together by the shore of a lake. For company, the two men talked and played with the birds and animals. They were friendly with them all—all, that is, except the treacherous Serpent People, the evil, giant snakes who lived beneath the water and tried to kill the kindly animals who were Nanabush's friends.

Nanabush and the Serpent People often fought with each other, and it was because of one of these fights that Nanabush made our world.

One winter day, Nanabush's brother was out hunting alone. When he did not come home in the evening, Nanabush thought that perhaps he had lost his way in the woods. The next day the young brother still had not returned, and Nanabush became worried. So he set out to try and find him. He had often warned his brother never to return home across the ice which covered the lake, but rather to walk around the shoreline on solid ground. He now began to fear that his brother had forgotten his warning and that he had been pulled through the ice by the Serpent People and drowned in the icy water below.

Nanabush searched everywhere, but not a trace of his brother could he find. He knew that the worst must have happened: the Serpent People had drowned his brother, as he had feared. He set out again, this time to find the Serpents and punish them.

Now the Serpent People were very cunning, and kept themselves well hidden. Nanabush tramped in vain through the woods and across the frozen rivers for days, and weeks, and months. Before he knew it, spring had come.

One day, just as he was approaching a steep hill, he heard a peculiar booming sound.

"What can that be?" he asked himself. "I must climb the hill and find out."

When he reached the top he saw a little lake in the valley below, and there, sunning themselves on the shore, were two Serpents. The booming noise came from the pounding of their giant hearts.

Quietly but swiftly, Nanabush drew his bow and shot an arrow at each Serpent. Though he hit them both, they were still very much alive, for they slithered into the water in the twinkling of an eye and disappeared.

Then a strange thing happened. The water in the little lake began to rise. It rose steadily, soon flooding the whole valley.

"Oho!" exclaimed Nanabush. "The Serpents know I am hunting them. They are going to try and drown me."

He climbed the tallest pine tree on the hill, but the water, which by this time had covered the hill, was lapping at his heels. He climbed as quickly as he could, and before long was at the very top of the tree. The water kept on rising and soon reached the level of his chin, but then strangely, the water began to go down again. It went down as quickly as it had risen, and when it had receded to its old level, Nanabush climbed down out of the pine tree.

"They nearly drowned me," said Nanabush, catching his breath. "I shall have to be careful, or next time those evil Serpents will certainly kill me."

He then chopped down a number of trees and made a giant raft, which he left on the top of the hill. Wondering what he should do next, he wandered away through the woods again. He had walked for nearly an hour when suddenly he stopped. He thought he could hear a woman crying. He crept on cautiously, and came to a clearing where an old woman was sitting on a log and, just as he had imagined, she was crying.

"Why are you crying, old woman?"

"Ah, a sad thing has happened. That wicked man, Nanabush, has wounded my brothers with his arrows."

Nanabush knew at once that the old woman was a Serpent Woman in disguise. He also realized that she did not know who he was.

Smiling to himself, he exclaimed, "That Nanabush must be a rascal! But tell me, what are you going to do?"

"I am gathering herbs to heal their wounds," she replied. "I am also gathering basswood bark. We shall twist the bark into a long string and stretch it around the base of the hill. We shall watch the string and if it vibrates, we shall know Nanabush tripped over it. He is hiding somewhere on the hill."

"Where do the Serpent People live?" he asked next.

"All you have to do is follow this path to the lake," replied the old woman, pointing the way. "When you get to the lake, walk right into it. A short distance in, you will find a door. The Serpent People are inside."

Without saying another word, Nanabush slew the wicked old Serpent Woman and dressed himself in her clothes. He followed the path to the lake and found the door. He opened it and found himself inside a huge lodge—the home of the Serpent People.

Walking along quickly, he soon came upon the two Serpents whom he had wounded, with his arrows still in their bodies. The serpents were guarded by a group of fierce animals, and Nanabush discovered that one of the Serpents he had wounded was the Chief of all the Serpents. However, the fierce animals thought Nanabush was the old woman, and let him pass.

In another corner, he saw the body of his brother, who had indeed been drowned by the Serpents. In a flash of anger, Nanabush leaped forward and pushed the arrows deeper into the bodies of the two Serpents, killing them instantly.

"Now I have avenged my brother's death!" he shouted. And, before the fierce guardian animals had time to realize what had happened, Nanabush slipped out of the Serpent lodge and raced back to the shore of the lake, running as fast as he could.

When the guardian animals realized what had happened they roared with rage and summoned the rest of the Serpent People, who immediately caused the water in the lake to rise again. But Nanabush heard the movement of the water as it began to rise, and he ran toward the hill where he had hidden his giant raft. As he ran he called loudly to his friends, the birds and animals.

"Come with me, my friends!" he shouted. "Come to my raft on the hill. The water is rising again, and this time you will drown unless you come with me."

The birds and animals answered his call not a moment too soon. Just as they reached the giant raft and climbed safely aboard, the water rose over the crest of the hill and set the raft afloat. In a few more minutes the whole world was covered by the surging water. There was not a single thing to be seen on the top of the water except Nanabush and the birds and animals on the raft. Even the highest hills were now lost from sight.

Nanabush and the birds and animals floated around aimlessly on the raft for many days and nights. At first Nanabush thought the water would go down again, but after they had been on the raft a full month he realized that the old world was submerged forever beneath the water and that the wicked Serpent People had drowned with it. Nanabush himself would have to find a way to create a new one.

"Loon!" he called, when he had decided what he should do. "You are an excellent swimmer. Dive down and bring me a lump of mud in your bill."

The loon dived into the water and was gone a long time. Presently, he returned.

"I couldn't reach the old world," he reported sadly. "It was too far down."

"Beaver!" called out Nanabush, "you are a good diver. You try next."

The beaver dived in and was gone much longer than the loon had been, but he too failed to reach the bottom of the vast ocean.

"Muskrat!" exclaimed Nanabush, "you must try for us."

The muskrat dived in and was gone for so long that they were certain he had drowned. Just as they were giving him up for lost, he suddenly appeared on the surface, motionless, floating around as if he were indeed dead.

Nanabush pulled the muskrat onto the raft and revived him. He noticed that the little animal was holding one paw tightly closed. He pried it open—and there were a few tiny, wet particles of sand. The muskrat had reached the old world after all!

Nanabush took the grains of sand and dried them carefully. He fashioned them into a tiny globe, on which he breathed lightly. Then he planted the globe gently on the water beside the raft, and commanded it to grow.

The little ball began to revolve and spin on the water, and soon it started to grow in size. Within a few minutes, it had grown large enough to hold two ants which Nanabush placed on it. The ants made the globe spin faster and grow bigger. In no time at all, it had grown large enough to hold two mice.

Thus it was that the little ball grew and grew. At last, when the moose—the largest of all animals—had climbed onto it and disappeared from sight, Nanabush commanded the globe to stop growing. He himself stepped onto it and said:

"Here is the new world—a home for all the birds and animals."

And that, so the Ojibwa storytellers say, is how Nanabush created the world in which we live today.

In the myths of many people, the process of creation is helped along by beings who seem to be part of the forces of nature, and who may be as destructive as they are creative. These are the tricksters.

Nanabush and Raven are both tricksters. Other trickster figures include Napi, Old Man, among the Blackfoot; Wee-sa-kay-jac among the Cree; Coyote in parts of the west, extending south as far as Mexico; and others. In other parts of the world, the African trickster Anansi the spider crossed to the West Indies with the Africans who were first taken there as slaves. Br'er Rabbit is another African trickster figure who crossed to the new world, where he lives on in the character of Bugs Bunny.

Tricksters are appealing because they combine weaknesses that seem human, such as pride, curiosity, greed, or mischievousness, with great power. They are clowns and creator gods at the same time. In many cultures tricksters are neither male nor female, but in English they are referred to as "he," so they have a probably unwarranted reputation for being usually male.

Coyote and the Fish Dam

BY CELIA BARKER LOTTRIDGE

If Coyote hadn't done what he did, his people would never have tasted salmon.

One day Coyote was crossing the Thompson River high up in the Rocky Mountains. His foot slipped on a wet log and he fell into the rushing stream. Now, Coyote was not a good swimmer, and he knew he would drown in that cold water if he didn't do something, so he changed himself into a piece of wood and went floating on down the river.

The Thompson River flowed into the Fraser River, and the piece of wood was carried into regions Coyote did not know at all. At dusk it stopped against a fish dam. Two women had built the dam to catch the salmon as they swam up the river. It was such a good dam that Coyote, living high in the mountains, had never seen or tasted salmon. All night long Coyote floated on the upstream side of the dam, content to be a piece of wood.

In the morning the two women came to see whether they had caught any salmon and one of them saw Coyote. "That is a good piece of wood," she said. "I will take it home and make it into a bowl." So she took the wood and shaped it into a bowl. Then she put salmon in the bowl and went about her work.

When she came to get some salmon for her evening meal, she found that half of the fish was gone. It looked as though something with sharp teeth had bitten it off. The woman put more salmon in the bowl and began to eat, but the fish disappeared so quickly that she could not get enough.

"This bowl is no use to me," she said, and she picked it up and threw it into the fire. Immediately she heard a baby cry. Both women stared at the fire, until one of them said, "If there is a baby in that fire I will keep it and raise it. I have always wanted to have a child."

She reached into the fire and lifted out a baby boy. He was a handsome child and he grew quickly, but he was headstrong and difficult to rear. Soon he was running all around the hut where the women lived, and playing down by the river. He was so mischievous that the women usually did not take him with them when they went into the forest to gather food. Instead they spoke to him and told him, "While we are away you may play in the house and down by the river, but you must never touch the four boxes we keep in the corner." The little boy would look at the four big carved wooden boxes and say nothing.

Every day Coyote went down to the river to look at the fish dam. He made up his mind that some day he would break that dam. He now knew how good salmon was to eat, and he knew how many salmon came swimming up the river to be caught at the dam. He wanted his people high up in the mountains to have the salmon too.

And every day Coyote looked at those four boxes, and he wondered what the women kept there. It must be something even better than the salmon.

One day the women told the boy they were going off to gather food. They told him again not to touch the four boxes. He said nothing, but they could tell he understood them.

When they had gone Coyote ran down to the river to look at the dam. He ran to the hut and looked at the four boxes. Then he ran back to the dam. But he had to know what was in those boxes, so he ran back and quickly pulled off all four lids. Out of one box came smoke wasps. Out of the next, salmon flies. Out of the next, blow flies, and out of the last, meat beetles.

Coyote ran to the river. He broke the fish dam. Then the salmon were swimming up the river, Coyote was running up the river, and after him were coming clouds of insects. And so it is to this day. When the salmon come up the rivers, the insects come too. All because of Coyote.

Anansi Gives Nyame a Child

COLLECTED BY
HAROLD COURLANDER

In this story, Anansi creates part of the reality we live in, even though he is motivated only by laziness and foolishness.

A nansi and Nyame the Sky God were friends. And it happened one time when they were in conversation that Nyame looked at his children and said, "See how all my children are the same color, all are dark."

Anansi said, "Yes, it is monotonous. I will bring you one of a different color."

Nyame replied, "Well, now, that is something. You make difficulties for yourself, but I will hold you to it."

Anansi left Nyame and went home, thinking, "Where shall I get Nyame a child of a different color?" He looked everywhere, but there were only children of dark complexion. Time passed. Nyame sent messengers to Anansi. They asked, "Where is the child you promised Nyame?" Anansi spoke to them as though he were offended. He said, "Does one make a baby instantly?" And when the messengers came again, Anansi answered, "Is a baby made in two months?" More time passed. The messengers again came, saying, "Nyame inquires about the child you promised him." Anansi replied, "Since when is a baby born in four months?" Anansi went on looking for a different-colored child. When the messengers from Nyame appeared another time at his house, eight months had passed. He told them: "Surely Nyame does not want a too-early child? The nine months are not yet used up."

Because Nyame had said, "I will hold you to it," Anansi became anxious. He decided to hide himself in the forest so that people would think he had died while hunting. He went out with his weapons and disappeared among the trees. He followed a trail used by hunters. He was gone a long while.

Now there was a woman from a distant village who had given birth to a boy child. The child's appetite was unending. Whatever she gave him, he wanted more. Her milk did not satisfy him. She gave him mush, but that did not fill his stomach. For seven days she devoted herself to feeding him from morning till night, but his hunger was never satisfied. At last she said, "This child is unnatural. He hungers without end. And his color is not the color of others. He is red. Surely this matter is too big to deal with." So she took the infant into the forest and placed him in the crotch of a tree, after which she went back to her village.

Anansi was walking along the game trail. He heard the crying of an infant. He found the baby where the mother had left it. He saw that its color was red, and he rejoiced, saying, "At last I can give birth." He took the baby home. He sent word to Nyame that the nine months were up and the child had been born. Nyame dispatched messengers to Anansi's house. They found Anansi lying on his mat as though he were recovering. He said: "Here, as I promised, is the child of a different color. Why does my friend Nyame reproach me? I have done what I promised."

The messengers took the child to Nyame's house. Nyame saw that its color was red instead of dark and he was pleased. He gave the baby to his senior wife, saying, "Take it, care for it as your own." She gave the child milk, but it cried for more. She asked Nyame's other wives for help. They all gave milk, they all fed the child mush, yet it continued to cry for more. At last Nyame's senior wife complained. She went to Nyame, saying, "It's an impossible thing. He does not stop wanting. He cries. He makes a great disturbance."

Nyame was annoyed. He said, "Whoever heard of such a thing?" But the child answered him. He said, "Where I lived before I ate better than here." So Nyame answered, "Very well." And he began to take care of the baby himself. He ordered milk brought. He ordered boiled plantains and other food. He began to feed the child. Whenever he stopped the child cried for more. Nyame sent word out into the village that all the people should bring food. They brought pots of everything. Whatever they brought, the boy was ready for it. People came from everywhere to watch him eat. Nyame's servants brought huge vessels of water so that the boy could wash down his food.

The food and water were gone. The boy looked in one direction and another. He saw that the feeding was ended. In the front of the crowd that was watching him an old man was standing, his mouth wide open in amazement. The boy jumped into his mouth. He became a tongue. It was the first tongue. Because the boy was red, all tongues are red. Because the boy was never satisfied, tongues are never satisfied. If a person's stomach is full or empty, it is all the same to his tongue. The tongue always wants something. So there is a saying, "Even though the stomach has plenty, the tongue wants more." For all this Anansi was responsible.

The Apples of Iduna

BY DOROTHY HOSFORD

Here, the Norse trickster Loki gets the gods into trouble, and then bails them out again.

The Norse were probably the first Europeans to land in North America. They were closely related to the English and the other Germanic peoples who settled across western Europe.

The Norse saw the universe as an immense tree on which everything rested: Asgard, the world of the gods; Midgard, or "Middle Earth," the world we live in; and Niflheim, the frozen underworld. The ancient Germans paid honors to sacred trees, which they saw as images of this World Tree.

The ruler of the gods was All-Father Odin. He was a warrior, the god of warriors and kings; he was also the god of bards and poets, and the great seeker of knowledge. Odin liked to travel between the worlds, appearing to people as a one-eyed old man in a blue cloak with a wide-brimmed hat. From Asgard, he saw all things from his air throne, attended by his wolves and his ravens, Thought and Memory.

Thor, god of thunder, son of Odin, was the great god of farmers. Quick-tempered, red-bearded, and immensely strong, he was also a reliable and kind-hearted friend of ordinary people. His hammer Miolnir was the strongest weapon of the gods: the dwarves made it for him, and it always came back to his hand after smashing anything it hit.

In the Norse myths, the gods were constantly at war with the giants, who lived in Jotunheim, the vast wilderness surrounding our world. The giants were dark elemental powers of the earth, something like the Greek Titans. The Norse believed that in the end fire giants and frost giants, storm giants and mountain giants, would join forces with all the powers of unbeing and sweep away the gods.

Within this central drama were many other powers—the goddesses Frigga and Freya, the war god Tyr, the gatekeeper Heimdall, the dwarves or dark elves, with their miraculous power to create—but Loki was in a category of his own. A descendant of the trickster figure, Loki was half giant and half god, an androgynous shape-shifter able to appear in any form. Often Odin's companion and almost his twin, Loki lived among the gods, and through his cleverness won for them many of their greatest gifts. But he was driven by a restless spirit, and eventually he became their greatest enemy.

In this myth, Odin and Loki go travelling with a third god, Hoenir, and encounter the storm giant Thiazi.

Odin often traveled forth from Asgard to take part in the affairs of men and to see what was going on in all the wide expanses of the world. One day he set out on such a journey, taking Loki and Hoenir with him. They wandered a long way over mountains and waste land, and at length they grew hungry. But food was hard to find in that lonely country.

They had walked many miles when they saw a herd of oxen grazing in a valley.

"There is food for us at last," said Hoenir.

They went down into the valley and it was not long before they had one of the oxen roasting on a fire. While their meal cooked they stretched out on the ground to rest. When they thought the meat had cooked long enough they took it off the fire. But it was not yet ready. So they put it back over the embers and waited.

"I can wait no longer," cried Loki at last. "I am starving. Surely the meat is ready."

The gods scattered the fire once more and pulled forth the ox, but it seemed as though it had not even begun to cook. It was certainly not fit for eating.

This was a strange thing and not even Odin knew the meaning of it. As they wondered among themselves, they heard a voice speak from the great oak tree above them.

"It is because of me," said the voice, "that there is no virtue in your fire and your meat will not cook."

They looked up into the branches of the tree and there sat a huge eagle.

"If you are willing to give me a share of the ox, then it will cook in the fire," said the eagle.

There was little the gods could do but agree to this. The eagle let himself float down from the tree and alighted by the fire. In no time at all the ox was roasted. At once the eagle took to himself the two hindquarters and the two forequarters as well.

This greediness angered Loki. He snatched up a great pole, brandished it with all his strength, and struck the eagle with it. The eagle plunged violently at the blow and whirled into the air. One end of the pole stuck fast to the eagle's back and Loki's hands stuck fast to the other end. No matter how he tried he could not free them. Swooping and turning, the eagle dragged Loki after him in his flight, flying just low enough that Loki's feet and legs knocked against stones and rock heaps and trees. Loki thought his arms would be torn from his shoulders. He cried out for mercy.

"Put me down! Put me down!" begged Loki. "Free me and you shall have the whole ox for your own."

"I do not want the ox," cried the eagle. "I want only one thing—Iduna and her apples. Deliver them into my power and I will set you free."

Iduna was the beautiful and beloved wife of the god Bragi. She guarded the most precious possession of the gods, the apples of youth. Unless they might eat of them the gods would grow old and feeble like mortal men. They kept the gods ever young. Iduna and her apples were priceless beyond words.

"Iduna and her apples! Such a thing cannot be done," shouted Loki.

"Then I will fly all day," screamed the eagle. "I will knock you against the rocks until you die." And he dragged Loki through rough tree branches and against the sides of mountains and over the rocky earth. Loki could endure it no longer.

"I will do as you ask," he cried. "I will bring Iduna to you, and her apples as well."

"Give me your oath," said the eagle. Loki gave his oath. A time was set when Loki should put Iduna in the eagle's power.

The eagle straightway made Loki free and flew off into the sky. A much-bruised Loki returned to his companions, and all three set off on their homeward journey. But Odin and Hoenir did not know the promise which Loki had made.

Loki pondered how he could keep his word to the eagle, whom he now knew to be the giant Thiazi in disguise. When the appointed day came Loki approached Iduna.

"Iduna," he said, speaking gently, "yesterday I found a tree on which grow wondrous apples. It is in the wood to the north of Asgard. They are like your apples in color and shape. Surely they must have the same properties. Should we not gather them and bring them to Asgard?"

"There are no apples anywhere," said Iduna, "like to my apples."

"These are," said Loki. "They are very alike. Come and look for yourself. If you bring your apples we can put them side by side and you will see."

So Iduna went with Loki to the wood, taking her apples with her. While they were in the wood the giant Thiazi swooped down in his eagle's plumage and carried Iduna and her apples off to his abode.

The gods soon missed Iduna. And they knew her apples were gone, for the signs of old age began to show among them. They grew bent and stiff and stooped.

Odin called a hasty council of the gods. They asked each other what they knew of Iduna.

"Where was she last seen?" asked Odin.

Heimdall had seen her walking out of Asgard with Loki. That was the last that was known of her.

Odin sent Thor to seize Loki and to bring him to the council. When Loki was brought the gods threatened him with tortures and death unless he told what he knew of Iduna. Loki grew frightened and admitted that Iduna had been carried off to Jotunheim.

"I will go in search of her," he cried, "if Freya will lend me her falcon wings."

Freya was more than willing. When Loki had put on the feather dress he flew to the north in the direction of Jotunheim.

He flew for a long time before he came to the home of Thiazi, the giant. Then he circled slowly overhead and saw Iduna walking below. She carried in her arms her golden casket of apples. Thiazi was nowhere to be seen, for he had rowed out to sea to fish. Loki quickly alighted on the ground beside Iduna.

"Hasten, Iduna," he cried, "I will rescue you." And he changed Iduna into the shape of a nut and flew off with her in his claws.

Loki had no sooner gone than Thiazi arrived home. At once he missed Iduna and her precious apples. Putting on his eagle's plumage, he flew into the air. Far off in the distance he saw the falcon flying. Instantly he took after him. The eagle's wings beat powerfully, making a deep rushing sound like a great wind. Thiazi drew nearer and nearer to Loki. Loki flew with all his might, but the eagle was bearing down upon the falcon just as the towers of Asgard came into view. With a last burst of strength Loki hastened toward the shining battlements.

The gods were on watch for Loki's return. They saw the falcon bearing the nut between his claws, with the eagle in close pursuit. Quickly they built a great pile of wood shavings just outside the wall of Asgard. As Loki came near he swooped down low over the shavings. Thiazi swooped down too, hoping to seize the falcon before he reached the safety of Asgard. Just as the eagle came close to the pile the gods set fire to the shavings. Instantly the fire blazed up, but Thiazi could not stop himself. He plunged into the flames and the feathers of his wings took fire. Then he could fly no more and the gods slew him where he was.

There was great rejoicing within the walls of Asgard to have Iduna safe once more. And the gods grew young and bright again.

Hermes, Lord of Robbers

TRANSLATED AND ADAPTED
BY PENELOPE PRODDOW

The Greek god Hermes is a trickster, too. Here is a translation of an ancient hymn to Hermes. It is a perfect trickster story: out of playfulness, Hermes creates the lyre, which he trades to Apollo, becoming the patron god of trade and commerce. He also becomes the patron god of thieves.

Muse, sing to me of Hermes, the son of Zeus and Maia.

Maia—a gentle nymph with flowing hair—beloved of Zeus,
stayed away from the company of the joyous gods,
preferring to dwell in a shadowy cave.
And yet, when the tenth month came about in heaven,
Maia gave birth.
And a most remarkable thing occurred. . . .

She bore a son—
crafty, of winning wiles,
a robber, a driver of cattle,
a bringer of dreams, a spy in the night,
a watcher at gates—who quickly was destined
to do glorious deeds among the immortals.
At dawn he was born. At midday he was playing the lyre.
In the evening, he stole the cows of far-shooting Apollo.

The moment Hermes came into being,
he would not remain in a hallowed cradle,
but, slipping out,
he started his search for Apollo's cattle.
Creeping over the threshold of the high-roofed cave,
he came across a tortoise.

The luck-bringing son of Zeus laughed with delight.
"This is a sign of great luck *for me*!
I will not be discourteous!
Good morning! Leader of the dance!
Shapely one! Companion at the feast!
Your presence is welcome.
And how did you, a tortoise dwelling in the hills,
get that rich finery for a wrap—
that gleaming shell? As long as you live,
you and your kind will ward off sorcery,
but when you die, then you will sing most sweetly."

So saying, Hermes fashioned the tortoise into a lyre.
And after he had finished,
lifting it high—that lovely toy—
he plucked each string in turn…
though in his heart he was thinking of other things.

Fondling the lyre,
he tucked it away in the sacred cradle,
then leaped from the fragrant chamber down to a rock
and pondered in his heart sheer villainy
such as knaves do on a pitch-black night.

The sun, with his steeds and chariot,
was disappearing beneath the earth
into the sea,
when Hermes came bounding up to Pieria,
the misty mountain of the gods.

Here, the celestial cattle had stalls
and fed on grassy, unmown meadows.
And there, Maia's child
cut off from the herd
fifty lowing cows.

He drove the lumbering beasts *backward* over a sandy plain—
so that their tracks would point the other way.
Then, planning a lengthy journey,
he plucked armfuls of fresh green wood,
and he tied them, leaves and all,
comfortably under his feet
as sandals.

An old man, digging a budding vineyard, saw him. . .
hurtling across the fields of Onchestus.

The moon had just stepped up to her watch place
when Zeus's robust son
hustled the broad-chested cattle of the god Apollo
up to the river Alpheus.
In excellent spirits,
they surged around the byres and watering troughs
that bordered a succulent meadow.

After the god had tended them,
he pitched his sandals into the foaming Alpheus
and at dawn
scampered back to the peaks of Mount Cyllene.

Not a soul saw him—
not a god,
not a mortal—
and not a dog barked.

The luck-bringing son of Zeus
swept sideways
through the keyhole in the hall
like an autumn breeze.

He could not glide past
the nymph his mother
and she spoke:
"Well, now! Cunning one!
Where have you come from
at this late hour
and in this manner—wearing shamelessness like a cloak?
I suspect Apollo will soon be here
to march you out of the door in fetters. . . ."

"Mother, why do you try to scare me
as though I were a helpless child?
I am seeking a craft
that will provide for us forever.
Of all the gods,
why should we live alone
without gifts and prayers, as you have done?
It is more desirable to move among the immortals all our days,
to be rich and prosperous, with ample cornfields,
than to sit at home in a dismal cave.

"If my father does not *give* me the honor,
I can succeed alone
in becoming the *Lord of Robbers*!
And if Apollo tracks me down,
another and more dire fate will befall him.
I will go to his mansion at Pytho and plunder it.
I will carry off tripods, fine cauldrons and gold—
that hoard of bright iron, and all his clothes!"

Dawn, giving light to men,
was rising from the ocean,
when Apollo came in haste to Onchestus.
There he found an old man, grazing his beast.
"Tell me, Ancient One,
have you seen a man pursuing cattle
along this road?"

The old man replied:
"It seemed—you must bear with me,
since I cannot say for sure—
that I saw... a child,
a mere infant, waving a staff.
He drove the cattle backward
with their heads toward him. . . ."

On hearing these words,
Apollo knew the thief was Hermes, child of Zeus.
Swiftly the god Apollo proceeded to sandy Pylos,
seeking his rolling-gaited cattle.
Spying the tracks, he exclaimed:
"Indeed! I have seen a great wonder!
These are the tracks of my fine-horned cattle,
going *backward*!
The footprints, however,
are not like those of man or woman,
of white wolves, lions or bears,
nor, do I believe,
of shaggy-necked centaurs—
whoever has with hastening feet
made such enormous strides!"

He streaked on
and came to the forest-clad mountain Cyllene
and the shadowy cave in the rock
where the divine nymph had given birth to Hermes.

Quickening his pace,
Apollo stepped over the stone threshold into the sombre cavern.
Quickly he peered into every corner of the dwelling—
then cried to glorious Hermes:
"Oh child, curled up in a cradle,
tell me this instant
the whereabouts of my cattle!"

Hermes lisped drowsily:
"Have you come here in search of common cattle?
Do I look like a stealer of cattle—a swaggering fellow?
Yesterday I was born.
my feet are tender, and the ground
beneath them is hard."

Apollo laughed ominously.
"Climb out of your cradle, comrade of dark night!"
So spoke Phoebus Apollo, and seized the baby.

Caught in Apollo's grasp,
Hermes sneezed wildly. . .
whereupon Apollo dropped him onto the ground.

Hermes leaped up, moving back in alarm.
"Give me my right of justice," he cried.
"Take me to Zeus!"

There was excitement on snow-capped Olympus.
The gods were assembling at dawn.

Cloud-gathering Zeus questioned his shining son:
"Where have you come from, Phoebus,
leading this great prize,
this newborn child, who looks like a bearer of tidings?"

"*He* stole my cows," said Apollo,
"and swept them away at twilight
along the shore of the thundering sea,
advancing straight for the port of Pylos. . . ."

Hermes declared to Zeus:
"*He* came to our home this morning seeking his shambling cattle.
He bade me confess to the theft
and swore to hurl me down to Tartarus—
an easy feat
since he is in the prime of youth
and I was born but yesterday.

"He can see for himself
that I do not look like a robber of cattle—a swaggering fellow.
Believe me... *Father*!
I did not bring the cattle home
or take them over our threshold.
I speak the truth!"

Zeus laughed out loud, watching the sly child
skilfully denying the theft of the cows.
Whereupon he ordered them both
to stop quarrelling and find the beasts.

Illustrious Hermes saw fit to obey.
And so, the radiant sons of Zeus
went off to the ford of the Alpheus.

While Hermes ran up to the byres,
urging the cattle into the light,
Apollo, glancing about him,
spotted two hides on a towering rock.
Furiously, he called out to Hermes:
"How were you able, scoundrel,
if you are as weak as you say, to slay two cows?
You needn't grow much larger, child of Maia."

Soon he was twisting wiry shoots of willow in his hands.
He would tie up Hermes with unbreakable bonds.
But the shoots wouldn't hold
and the bonds slipped down.
They immediately started
to sprout from the ground and blossom around their feet.
Twining in and out, lightly they garlanded every one of the cattle—
because of clever Hermes.

Swiftly, Hermes soothed the son of Leto,
for Apollo was mightier than he.
He raised the lyre onto his left arm
and plucked each string in turn.
At his touch, it responded sweetly.

Phoebus Apollo smiled
and the soft notes of the godlike tune
went through his heart.

Hermes, gathering courage,
stole up to his left hand, playing skilfully.
And—all at once—he burst into song.
He sang of the deathless gods
reigning over the dark-black earth,
of their beginnings, and how each received his portion.

Longing overcame Apollo.
"Such music is worth fifty cows!" he cried.
"Has that magnificent object been yours since birth,
or did one of the gods or mortals make you that priceless gift?
Never have I cared for anything as much as I care for this!
I am astonished, child of Zeus, at your harmonies.
You will be famous shortly in the throng of immortals—
you and your mother. I speak the truth!"

Hermes replied slyly:
"I am not unhappy that you have discovered my skill.
Since you wish to play the lyre,
Sing!... Play!... Enjoy the gift of melting song—
receiving it *from me*."

Hermes gave him the lyre.
Phoebus Apollo accepted it eagerly
and placed his bright whip into Hermes' hands,
making him the Keeper of Cattle.

Raising the lyre upon his left arm,
the radiant son of Leto, the Lord, Far-working Apollo,
touched each string in turn.
Awesomely it rang, and the god sang wonderingly to the sound.

Apollo exclaimed joyously: "I shall give you also
the wonderful, golden, three-leafed staff of riches and wealth.

Accept this, child of Maia,
and the curling-horned cattle of the field.
Take charge of horses and steadfast mules,
bright-eyed lions, white-toothed boars,
dogs and sheep and all the flocks ...."

Thus, Apollo showed his devotion to Maia's child in many ways—
and Hermes promised in turn
he would never carry off anything the Far-shooter owned,
nor would he rob his huge house.

Now, Hermes mingles with both the mortals and immortals.
He profits, of course...
As on down through the dark nights,
he tricks the tribes of men.

The Childhood of Krishna

The theme of creative power as a wilful child is a common one. Another good example, this time from the vast mythology of India, is the childhood of Krishna. Krishna was one of the incarnations that Vishnu, Lord of the existing Universe, takes from time to time to appear among his creation.

Krishna was born in a village of poor cattle herders. Even though he was the Master of the Universe, playing at being a human child, he was naughty sometimes. The villagers complained to his mother that the little boy played tricks on them.

One day his mother Yasoda called him inside to scold him, because he had been seen eating dirt from the ground. With thumb and forefinger she stretched his mouth wide open, looking within to find the dirt. And inside his mouth she saw the whole universe open out: the sun and moon and stars, stretching out in night and space; the oceans and the continents, and all the forms of life; the lightening and the rain and sunlight; all things past and all to come. She fell into amazement, wondering at the Being of her son; until he, in mercy, cast an illusion of forgetfulness and appeared again as her little boy upon her knee.

How the Raven Lost His Beak

BY BILL REID AND
ROBERT BRINGHURST

One time the Raven ran afoul of the Big Fisherman, who tried to kill him by pounding him to a pulp and throwing him into the sea. This Haida story concentrates on the funny side of the trickster. Poor whale, though . . .

The Raven, or what was left of him—a wad of ruptured organs, crushed bones and broken body parts bound together with fishing line and weighted with heavy stones—sank swiftly into the bottomless trench in the seabed which the Big Fisherman had selected as the likeliest place to dispose of this troublesome creature once and for all.

But of course there was no real danger of that. The Raven is doomed to continue forever his restless wanderings through the world, searching for something to quell his insatiable appetites. Sinking endlessly into a bottomless pit in the sea is a fate no worse than many others, but the Raven knew he must put it behind him sooner or later. So instead of vanishing into the infinite depths of the ocean, from which it could be laborious to emerge, the Raven transformed himself quickly once more. With tremendous effort, he reconstituted the broken shreds of his body, rebuilding them not into his usual glossy black shape, but into the form of a silver-bright, sleek spring salmon.

With a quick shake of his lithe new body, he was able to free himself of the fishing line and the stones. He began at once swimming back upward toward the world of sunlight and air—the world in which, like the rest of his kind, he was most comfortable and with which he was most familiar.

Nearing the bright canopy of waves, the Raven was contemplating quite cheerfully his immediate prospects and savoring memories of the pleasanter parts of his recent adventures. These thoughts occupied him sufficiently that he failed to notice the huge black-and-white form of the great hunter, one of the lords of the water universe, a *sghana*, or killer whale, bearing swiftly down upon him. When he felt the great jaws open behind him at last, escape was clearly impossible. In the final moment before the teeth clashed shut upon him, he turned and swam up the long black tunnel of the throat, into the cavernous belly of the whale.

Seeing that his salmon shape had clearly outlived its usefulness, the Raven resumed his usual form—eyes, beak, feathers, and claws all as black as the starless night in which he was born.

It was warm and, for a moment, somewhat restful deep in the body of the killer whale. It was better than lying, trussed up in fishing line in the bottom of the Big Fisherman's canoe, and certainly better than being bitten in half and chewed. But when his eyes began to smart and the ends of his feathers to wilt and fray in the strong stomach acids of the whale, the Raven concluded it was time to leave. Drawing, therefore, on his most basic natural powers, he pecked and clawed his way through the walls of the whale's belly and out through the layers of muscle, blubber, and hide.

After all this profitless activity, one would think that the Raven would stop for nothing on his way back to his natural element. But the Raven is not an altogether prudent sort of bird, and after the unexpected labor of chewing a hole in the side of the whale, the Raven had been reminded that he was hungry. So when a tasty-looking bit of octopus tentacle drifted by, as it did just then, within easy range of his beak, he reached out and grabbed it.

He should have suspected, of course, that a carefully cut and skinned section of octopus tentacle floating near the sea floor might not have been placed there for the express delectation of underwater ravens hatched from the bellies of passing killer whales. All things considered, he ought to have looked the piece of tentacle over quite carefully before gobbling it down—but when food is at hand, the Raven often forgets such precautions.

So he failed to notice the strip of kelp leading down to the stone sinker on the ocean floor below the tentacle, and he failed to notice the second strand of kelp leading up from the stone toward the surface. He failed to notice the hook, too, until the barb stabbed suddenly into his upper beak and his body was flooded with pain.

This pain was compounded a moment later, as the Raven was suddenly flipped on his back and began to lurch helplessly toward the surface. He had been caught, as he now knew, by one of the ingenious halibut hooks of the Haidas, which flip the fish over as soon as the hook sets and tension is put on the line. In this way, the flow of water over the gills is reversed, and before it is drawn to the surface, the halibut drowns.

If the Raven, so skilled as he is at holding his breath, was himself in no great danger of drowning, he was nevertheless in excruciating pain, and he could expect in a few more moments to be at the mercy of mere human beings, and to suffer still further humiliation and pain at their hands. When he saw that the current had brought him in reach of a kelp bed, he lunged for one of the largest stalks and hung onto it fiercely with his claws. The halibut fishermen in their canoe struggled meanwhile to bring in their suddenly obstinate catch, and a vigorous tug-of-war ensued. Neither Raven nor fisherman nor fishline nor kelpstalk would yield, and at last the whole upper beak of the desperate bird was torn out of his face by its roots and jerked toward the surface.

The Raven clung to the kelp for some moments in agony, wondering how he would ever be able to eat properly again. Then he rose to the surface at last and flew high into the air, watching the fishermen paddle away. He followed them to their camp in a small cove where they beached their canoe and kindled a fire. Once he was satisfied they would be there all evening, he flew back out to sea in the fading light, looking for anything that would help him recover his beak, and when his sharp ears heard it, he knew what he was seeking: the mournful peal of the wounded killer whale.

Flying in short circles over the stricken animal, the Raven spoke to him in tones of great sympathy.

"Alath, my poor friend," said the Raven with the broken beak, "I thee that you altho are in great dithtreth, and I fear that if both of uth do not get help we will quickly perith.

"I am going now to the houthe of a great thaman [shaman], whothe powerth I have ekthperienthed before. You may follow me if you with, and I will athk him to treat you too."

The astonished whale thanked the Raven profusely and readily agreed.

"He ith ekthpecting me only," said the Raven. "Wait a little dithtanth offthyore, and I will tell him you are there. If he agreeth to treat you, I will thignal you by throwing dry thedar onto the fire."

Again the suffering whale agreed.

"When you thee the fire blathe up, you mutht come athyore. The thaman can only treat you on the beach. You mutht thwim right up through the thallowth and onto the gravel, ath clothe ath pothible to the fire."

And so desperate, yet so hopeful, was the whale, that he agreed unquestioningly even to these instructions.

The Raven perched on his dorsal fin, guiding him toward the camp, and when they came up opposite the cove, where the fire could be clearly seen, the whale slowed.

"Wait here," said the Raven to the whale, and he flew alone to the edge of the beach.

As he landed, he transformed himself once more, now taking the form of a shrivelled little human being. Even in human form, he was missing his nose and most of his palate. To obscure this deformity, he transformed his cloak of feathers into an oversized spruceroot hat, which covered his whole face and most of his upper body, and in this guise he started toward the fire.

The fishermen, who had finished their evening meal, sat in a half circle around the flames, with their backs to the gentle evening breeze. They were discussing the day's events and passing from hand to hand the strange black object they had pulled out of the ocean. Each offered his own opinion of the catch, but in spite of their vast knowledge of the sea, not one of them could identify what it was, and none had a guess which seemed convincing to the others.

They were about to give up the discussion, for it was time to turn in for the night, when they heard slow footsteps coming toward them over the beach gravel. A small, wizened man—or at least they thought it was probably human—wearing a huge spruceroot hat and leaning on a walking stick, stepped into view in the dwindling firelight.

"I think I know what you have there," said a strange voice which came from under the hat, "but I'll have to ekthamine it clothely to be thyure."

Though he was small enough to seem harmless, such a suspicious looking creature, arriving so late at night, would normally have drawn a hostile reaction from the men around the fire. But his offer to answer the question which had perplexed them for several hours was enough that they invited him to sit down. One of them handed the visitor the beak, and he seemed to study it with great care.

"Yeth, I think tho," said the Raven. "Throw thome of that dry thedar on the fire, tho I can thee thith object more clearly."

The fisherman nearest the woodpile grabbed an armload of dry cedar sticks and tossed them onto the fire.

"Juth ath I thought," said the Raven, as the fresh flames rose. "I have theen one of theeth before, and it wath a bad day indeed for thothe who found it. Like you, they pathed it from hand to hand ath they that round the fire, contaminating themthelveth with the evil magic it contained. That night, though it wath ath calm ath it ith now, a great monthter came thuddenly out of the thea. It dethroyed their camp, their canoeth, and killed everyone ekthept me. I wath wounded, but I thurvived becauthe I fled into the foretht to hide. If I had run farther into the treeth, I might not have been injured, but I wath curiouth. I thtopped and looked back for a moment, and the monther'th power touched me."

As the Raven finished speaking, the beach behind him erupted with flying pebbles and spray. Using the last of his strength, the killer whale flung himself up on the gravel, roaring in agony at those gathered around the fire.

The fishermen leaped to their feet and ran into the forest, not once looking back, and the Raven chuckled maliciously as he heard the confused sounds of their frantic thrashing recede. Reassuming his natural form, he slid the beak back into place, and in moments it knitted there, strong and sound as though it had known no injury.

Thus equipped, and completely at leisure, he gorged himself on the ample supply of fresh halibut which the fishermen had left behind—and on the tasty and unarmed pieces of octopus tentacle which he found in their bait box. Temporarily satisfied, he flew off, bidding a contemptuous, lisping farewell to the dying whale.

As dawn broke, the fishermen made their way cautiously back to the beach, where they found their fire dead, their catch eaten or spoiled, and the stranger gone. A sad morning indeed, had they not also found on the beach, stranded by the falling tide, the dead killer whale.

The Haidas never hunted the whale themselves, but from that morning to this, they have eaten its flesh with great pleasure whenever they find a fresh killer whale carcass on shore.

So quite inadvertently once again, in the undivided pursuit of his calling—in the relentlessness of his search for amusement and food—the Raven had brought a little pleasure, a little profit and even some knowledge to his favorite playthings, human beings.

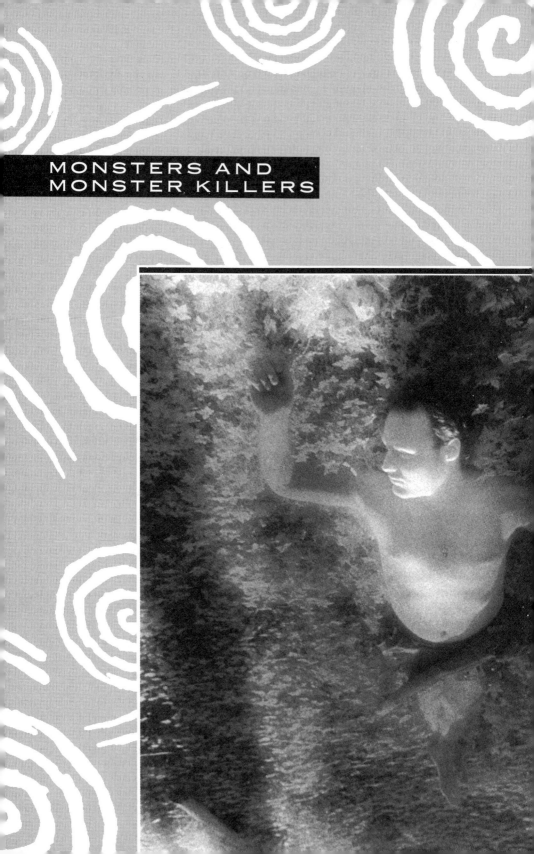

MONSTERS AND
MONSTER KILLERS

Since the earliest times human beings have feared the darkness. Over hundreds of thousands of years, our ancestors must have huddled by the fire together against the long night, against the wild animals they feared and had names for, and against the fears for which they had no names.

People create stories to give shape to their deepest fears, so those fears can be conquered. Then out of their own imaginings they create heroes like themselves to defeat the monsters. These heroes differ greatly from each other, but in order to win they must have special qualities—perhaps a divine parent, or the power and cleverness of a trickster, or the help of a supernatural being. And when those heroes triumph, they remind us that we can conquer the terrors inside and outside ourselves.

Beowulf and the Fight with Grendel

BY ROSEMARY SUTCLIFF

Beowulf *is a hero story of the Anglo-Saxons.*

Hrothgar [Roger], King of the Danes, had built a great hall called Heorot where his people could feast and be entertained with tales of bravery and beauty. But from the beginning Heorot was haunted by the Night-Stalker Grendel, a monster who could not be harmed by any weapon: each night he came up with the sea-mists, to devour anyone within the hall.

Then Beowulf, a prince of the Geats, came to Hrothgar and swore that he would kill the monster Grendel. The Danes and Beowulf's Geats gathered in Heorot for a feast, and Hrothgar's queen offered round the mead jar.

And when the King had drunk, she carried the cup from one to another of the warriors, Geat and Dane alike, all down the benches, while one of her women coming behind with the mead jar refilled for her as often as the cup grew low. Last of all she came to Beowulf where he sat as guest of honor between her two sons. "Greeting, and joy be to you, Beowulf son of Ecgtheow; and all the thanks of our hearts, that you come so valiantly to our aid."

Beowulf rose to his feet and took the cup as she held it out to him. "Valor is a word to use when the battle is over," he said, smiling. "Give us your thanks, great Queen, when we have done the thing which we come to do. But this at least I promise you, that if we fail to rid you of the monster, we shall not live to carry home our shields." And throwing back his head, he drained the cup and gave it again into her hands.

But now the shadows were gathering in the corners of the hall, and as the daylight faded, a shadow seemed to gather on the hearts of all men there, a shadow that was all too long familiar to the Danes. Then Hrothgar rose in his High Seat, and called Beowulf to him again.

"Soon it will be dusk," he said, when the young Geat stood before him. "And yet again the time of dread comes upon Heorot. You are still determined upon this desperate venture?"

"I am not wont to change my purpose without cause," Beowulf said, "and those with me are of a like mind, or they would not have taken ship with me from Geatland in the first place."

"So. Keep watch, then. If you prevail in the combat before you, you shall have such reward from me as never yet heroes had from a King. I pray to the All-Father that when the light grows again out of tonight's dark, you may stand here to claim it. Heorot is yours until morning." And he turned and walked out through the postern door, a tall old man stooping under the burden of his own height, to his sleeping quarters, where Wealhtheow the Queen had gone before him.

All up and down the hall men were taking leave of each other, dwindling away to their own sleeping places for the night. The thralls [slaves] set back the benches and stacked the trestle boards against the gable-walls, and spread out straw-filled bolsters and warm wolfskin rugs for the fifteen warriors. Then they too were gone, and Heorot was left to the band of Geats, and the dreadful thing whose shadow was already creeping towards them through the dark.

"Bar the doors," Beowulf said, when the last footsteps of the last thrall had died away. "Bars will not keep him out, but at least they may give us some warning of his coming."

And when two of them had done his bidding, and the seldom-used bars were in their sockets, there was nothing more that could be done.

For a little, as the last fire sank lower, they stood about it, sometimes looking at each other, sometimes into the glowing embers, seldom speaking. Not one of them had much hope that he would see the daylight again, yet none repented of having followed their leader upon the venture. One by one, the fourteen lay down in their harness, with their swords beside them. But Beowulf stripped off his battle-sark and gave it with his sword and boar-crested helmet to Waegmund his kinsman and the dearest to him of all his companions, for he knew that mortal weapons were of no use against the Troll-kind; such creatures must be mastered, if they could be mastered at all, by a man's naked strength, and the red courage of his heart.

Then he too lay down, as though to sleep.

In the darkest hour of the spring night Grendel came to Heorot as he had come so many times before, up from his lair and over the high moors, through the mists that seemed to travel with him under the pale moon; Grendel, the Night-Stalker, the Death-Shadow. He came to the foreporch and snuffed about it, and smelled the man-smell, and found that the door which had stood unlatched for him so long was barred and bolted. Snarling in rage that any man should dare attempt to keep him out, he set the flat of his talon-tipped hands against the timbers and burst them in.

Dark as it was, the hall seemed to fill with a monstrous shadow at his coming; a shadow in which Beowulf, half springing up, then holding himself in frozen stillness, could make out no shape nor clear outline save two eyes filled with a wavering greenish flame.

The ghastly corpse-light of his own eyes showed Grendel the shapes of men as it seemed sleeping, and he did not notice among them one who leaned up on his elbow. Laughing in his throat, he reached out and grabbed young Hondscio who lay nearest to him, and almost before his victim had time to cry out, tore him limb from limb and drank the warm blood. Then, while the young warrior's dying shriek still hung upon the air, he reached for another. But this time his hand was met and seized in a grasp such as he had never felt before; a grasp that had in it the strength of thirty men. And for the first time he who had brought fear to so many caught the taste of it himself, knowing that at last he had met his match and maybe his master.

Beowulf leapt from the sleeping bench and grappled him in the darkness; and terror broke over Grendel in full force, the terror of a wild animal trapped; so that he thought no more of his hunting but only of breaking the terrible hold upon his arm and flying back into the night and the wilderness, and he howled and bellowed as he struggled for his freedom. Beowulf set his teeth and summoned all his strength and tightened his grip until the sinews cracked; and locked together they reeled and staggered up and down the great hall. Trestles and sleeping benches went over with crash on crash as they strained this way and that, trampling even through the last red embers of the dying fire; and the very walls seemed to groan and shudder as though the stout timbers would burst apart. And all the while Grendel snarled and shrieked and Beowulf fought in silence save for his gasping breaths.

Outside, the Danes listened in horror to the turmoil that seemed as though it must split Heorot asunder; and within, the Geats had sprung from their sleeping benches sword in hand, forgetful of their powerlessness against the Troll-kind, but in the dark, lit only by stray gleams of balefire from the monster's eyes, they dared not strike for fear of slaying their leader, and when one or other of them did contrive to get in a blow, the sword blade glanced off Grendel's charmed hide as though he were sheathed in dragon scales.

At last, when the hall was wrecked to the walls, the Night-Stalker gathered himself for one last despairing effort to break free. Beowulf's hold was as fierce as ever; yet none the less the two figures burst apart—and Grendel with a frightful shriek staggered to the doorway and through it, and fled wailing into the night, leaving his arm and shoulder torn from the roots in the hero's still unbroken grasp.

Beowulf sank down sobbing for breath on a shattered bench, and his fellows came crowding round him with torches rekindled at the scattered embers of the fire; and together they looked at the thing he held across his knees. "Not even the Troll-kind could live half a day with a wound such as that upon them," one of them said; and Waegmund agreed. "He is surely dead as though he lay here among the benches."

"Hondscio is avenged, at all events," said Beowulf. "Let us hang up this thing for a trophy, and a proof that we do not boast idly as the wind blows over."

So in triumph they nailed up the huge scaly arm on one of the roof beams above the High Seat of Hrothgar.

The first thin light of day was already washing over the moors, and almost before the grisly thing was securely in place the Danes returned to Heorot. They came thronging in to beat Beowulf in joyful acclaim upon his bruised and claw-marked shoulders, and gaze up in awe at the huge arm whose taloned fingers seemed even now to be striving to claw down the roof beam. Many of them called for their horses, and followed the blood trail that Grendel had left in his flight up through the tilled land and over the moors until they came to the deep sea-inlet where the monster had his lair, and saw the churning waves between the rocks all fouled and boiling with blood. Meanwhile others set all things on foot for a day of rejoicing, and the young men wrestled together and raced their horses against each other, filling the day with their merrymaking, while the King's harper walked to and fro by himself under the apple trees, making a song in praise of Beowulf ready for the evening's feasting which this night would not end when darkness fell.

Heracles and the Hydra

BY LEON GARFIELD
AND EDWARD BLISHEN

Heracles was the greatest of the Greek heroes.

I. The Punishment

Zeus was his father, and the Fates ruled that his life would be one of suffering, but that his deeds would be remembered forever. The Romans later called him Hercules, but his real name is Heracles. It means "the glory of Hera," yet the goddess Hera was his deadly enemy. Even before he was born, she tricked Zeus into giving the high kingship of Mycenae, which he had intended for Heracles, to his cowardly cousin Eurystheus. Then she sent two snakes to kill the infant Heracles where he lay sleeping in his crib. The little boy laughed and strangled them: this was his first deed of strength.

The hero grew to manhood, and lived in Thebes with his wife and children. Already famous for his deeds, he lived like any young married man. Then Hera sent a curse of madness on him. In his madness his young children appeared to him as snakes, and so he murdered them. Later, he awoke to horror at his deed.

Where could he go to beg forgiveness, or to forgive himself? Heracles came at last to the oracle at Delphi, one of the holiest places in Greece.

He came to it early one morning, a steep, quiet place between wooded mountains. Poised amid the dark trees above him was a shrine, a colonnaded nest for flying gods. He had reached Delphi, and before him was the temple of Apollo.

He crouched in the stunted grass, remaining motionless for many hours, while he summoned up courage to enter the temple and beg such a punishment from the gods that would balance out the horror of his crime. By now his anguish had lost some of its sharpness and sunk to a dull, leaden ache which his cramped position seemed to ease.

Little by little he became absorbed in a small patch of ground where a nation of insects were toppling hither and thither, bearing tiny boulders of dust to raise walls, palaces and temples in a country an arm's length off. He fell to wondering if they could see his huge face, and if his eyes were their gray skies with two black suns glaring down? Was this a great occasion for them, to be remembered for generations? Perhaps even now they were praying to him to be forgiven their insect sins. Great Face, what must we do to atone? Shall we catch a huge fierce bee and offer it up to you? Shall we build you a temple as high as the tallest blade of grass?

At last, Heracles rose; he was ready to enter the temple and learn his punishment. His state was dream-like; he scarcely saw the priestess who greeted him as a son of Zeus. He sighed; much good the divine seed had done him. Perhaps, even, it was the conflict between his divine and mortal parts that had made him mad?

"What must I do?"

"Leave Thebes, Heracles. Go to Mycenae and serve Eurystheus. Do whatever he bids you."

Heracles bowed his head. There had been a time when such a command would have filled him with anger and shame and seemed the end of the world; but now it was ant-like in proportion to his guilt.

The priestess spoke again. "He will set you twelve labors, Heracles. These you must endure."

"What labors can such a man as Eurystheus devise that would purify me of my crime? What can his spirit know of mine?"

But to this there was no answer, and Heracles left the temple of Apollo as sombrely as he had entered it. He turned his steps towards Mycenae and the beginning of his Labors.

The King of Mycenae was a man of taste; the very set of his lips and the slight but continual working of his mouth suggested he was always tasting—and hadn't really made up his mind whether anything was good or bad. Not even his wife escaped this cultured, critical air of his; consequently she wore a tight-lipped smile that suggested she had even more refined opinions of her own.

"So, Heracles, the gods have chosen me to decide upon your punishment." Eurystheus, seated high, gazed down on the young man the gods had delivered into his hands. Travel-stained and smeared with grief, Heracles returned his cousin's look, then lowered his eyes.

"Twelve labors you are to set me, Lord Eurystheus . . . ."

The king's mouth worked meditatively as he savored the pleasure of his situation; while the queen beside him smiled her tight-lipped smile at the bronze floor, the rich hangings, the absorbed servants and her own neat hands.

"He must be kept from children," said this queen, who, above all things, desired to show that she thought of matters her husband might have overlooked. Heracles's eyes blazed with sudden tears; the queen nodded with satisfaction; she had drawn first blood.

"You are strong, Heracles," said Eurystheus, with a knowledgable, considered air, "and we must make clever use of your strength, eh? And you have experience in, for want of a better word shall we say, murdering? So I would have you murder something for me, Heracles. But not a child, or a teacher; you have already shown how easily you can manage that. . . hmm?"

Eurystheus paused; he watched the young man with refined curiosity—as if he was observing some rare species of insect writhing in interesting pain.

"Yes. I would have you kill the great lion of Nemea, Heracles." He smiled. "Thus one pest shall rid the world of another, eh? And who cares which butchers which!"

"And the skin," put in the queen. "Let him flay the lion and bring back the skin. Else how shall we know whose blood is on his hands?"

The King of Mycenae glanced at his wife; and for once there was a cautious admiration in his eyes.

"Goodbye, Heracles. May the gods go with you. . .for assuredly you need watching, eh?"

II. The Hydra

Heracles killed the monstrous Nemean lion, a creature whose skin could not be pierced by any weapon. Only its own claw was sharp enough to flay its skin, and after that the hero wore the lion's skin around his shoulders, a symbol of his ferocity and an armor against all weapons. For his next labor, the cowardly Eurystheus commanded Heracles to kill the Lernian Hydra, a serpent-headed monster, poisonous beyond all healing.

Accompanied by his young nephew Iolaus, Heracles entered the dismal swamps of Lerna. All day they struggled onward through the underbrush, past bogholes that gave off a heavy, sickly smell. As the sun set and the sky darkened, a mist full of deceiving mirages rose from the ground, lit only by the flaring torch carried by Iolaus.

Onward movement now became hazardous; the firm places had been steadily diminishing until, quite suddenly, they came to an end. Heracles and Iolaus halted. Before them stretched a wide area—a lake—of gently moving slime; upon this smooth surface, dimly visible in the cloying mist, stood a tall figure and a shorter one, holding aloft a flaming torch. The remoteness and silence of the vision was very striking; in several places about the feet of the phantom images, soft, slow bubbles rose up and burst, discharging the heavy sweetish smell that was a characteristic of the entire region.

"Fire," whispered Heracles. "Give me fire." The heavy secrecy of the place oppressed all sound, so that even the whisper intruded sharply.

The torch was thrust towards him, dangerously close to his eyes. Through the veils of flame he saw Iolaus's face; he looked aside and touched the fire with an arrow head till the pitch ran over the bronze and the arrow was aflame. Then he sent it flaring into the misty swamp to meet its swift reflection and vanish with a sudden hiss. Three more burning arrows followed, arching over the quiet slime; and multiplied reflections, racing across the surface and flying out of the curtained air, turned the night into an angry design of loosely threading fire. Then all rushed to extinction—the threads of fire, the reflected torchlight, and the shadowy figures together. It was as if the arrows of Heracles had extinguished a dream.

The darkened mist swirled; heads came through it—flat, gleaming heads sistering each other on rocking necks. Twisting deeply together, these necks united in a wider vessel in which they throbbed like swollen veins.... It was the Hydra; silently it had kept pace behind the mist, casting back the phantom reflections from its glass-smooth skin.

"Iolaus," breathed Heracles, "set the trees afire . . . ."

Iolaus hesitated, then with a last look at Heracles and the nine heads rocking out of the mist, fled with his torch streaming high. As he ran, tearing the brand through invisible obstructions, storms of sparks rushed down, stinging his cheeks and arms; he heard twigs and branches begin to spit and crackle. The night trembled into a sullen redness, throwing into striking relief the shapes made by smoke pouring down through the interstices of the flaring trees. Such shapes, deformed and bulkily crimson, looked like the hidden thoughts of the air itself to which the smoke had given tell-tale substance.

Suddenly, over and above the spiteful clamor of the fire, Iolaus heard a violent crashing noise; but terror prevented him looking back. He fancied he heard a cry, but even then he ran on, driven by an overmastering feeling of disgust.

"Iolaus!"

The voice was wild and shaking. The boy hesitated; then against all his pressing instincts, he turned.

The Hydra had come out of the swamp. He saw it between the trees, huge and shining in the irregular firelight. Its extremities, numerous and flexible as its nest of necks, were twined about Heracles who seemed unable to move. Its nine heads jostled his face, which was turned towards Iolaus with a look of such mortal anguish that the boy forgot the last of his fears of Heracles.

An immense distress and pity seized him as he watched the world's great hero being slowly murdered by the stench and filth of the Hydra. Why was Heracles so still? Why were his great arms hanging limply as if he was already dead? Bewildered, Iolaus blundered towards the engulfing Hydra, crying out, "Fight back! For pity's sake, fight back!"

Heracles saw him. "Go...go...." he wept; then other heads came between him and Iolaus. The heads Heracles saw on the Hydra's necks were the heads of the children he'd slaughtered in the courtyard at Thebes. They smiled at him, jostled close for kisses.... Why were they so cold?

Madness in reverse had taken hold of him; he saw children where there were snakes. Such was the power of the Hydra that it caused each man to fight against himself—and then consumed him in forgetful slime. This was the testing time of Heracles, facing the vengeance of his deepest dreads. He felt his chest being squeezed and squeezed; his lungs were choked with evil smells; and his beloved sons opened their rosy mouths to give him nipping bites with teeth as bright as pearls.

"Strike at it! Strike at it!" cried Iolaus.

Heracles shuddered; he raised his arm—but not the one that held his club—and caressed the eager cheeks and stroked the obstinately tangled heads.

"Strike them off!" screamed Iolaus.

The flames leaped and crackled; branches crashed—and eyes like clustering stars rocked and danced in the air.

"The madness," groaned Heracles. "*This* is the madness!"

He lifted the hand that held his club, and gave a cry as if begging forgiveness; then he struck with all his might at the beloved heads. Whole trees roared into fire, holding up their branches as if to ward off the intense heat. Again and again Heracles struck—and the heads fell like rotten fruit with black blood gushing from the ruptured necks.

Iolaus shouted out in triumph—then his voice died. The black blood bubbled and crusted even as it flowed; and out of the crust rose new heads—two on every neck, and then two again as each of these new-born heads fell to Heracles' club. A hundred Hydras sprouted from the one; a teeming multitude of snakes waved about Heracles, like the stamens of some huge, gray flower. . . .

"Burn out the necks! Use the torch, Iolaus! The necks—sear them!"

Iolaus crept close; a head fell, cold and wet against his foot. He leaped back in horror—but then advanced again, holding out the torch till it found the blinded neck. He touched it with the dripping pitch; it hissed and shrank, then dropped like a length of dirty rope.

"The necks—the necks!" panted Heracles. So Iolaus found them; the dark blood boiled and steamed, the flesh shriveled and the dead necks fell in loose disarray. Little by little the crowding heads diminished—like a multitude departing—as the club of Heracles thrashed among them and Iolaus's fire scalded the stumps. Vague heaps of them glimmered on the ground like a windfall from an eerie tree . . . but all the while there was one head that did not fall: the head that contained the Hydra's brain. In vain Heracles battered at it, but it continued to lunge and dance and while it lived, the grip about Heracles grew tighter and tighter. . . .

Suddenly he felt a terrible pain in his foot. He glanced down. A crab had crawled from the swamp and had seized hold of his heel. Secure in its shell that must have seemed a mighty fortress, it had crawled to the aid of its monstrous companion from the slime: a scavenging Iolaus to its Heracles foul as sin.

He shouted in anger at the mockery and stamped the crab to fragments. Then he looked up. The Hydra's last head was close to his own. No maddened illusion now, no false image, but the flat, bland countenance of poison itself. Heracles saw himself deformed in its cold eyes. He saw appalling knowledge in its slow, gaping smile, knowledge of his darkest self—and of darkness everywhere. Knowledge without wisdom, without pity, without light.

"My sword, Iolaus! Give me my sword—"

The Hydra's jaws widened. Heracles, with the precision of extreme fear, saw venom bubbling in its throat, saw its divided tongue flicker and plunge . . . .

"Quickly! The sword!"

He dropped his club and stretched out his hand. He felt the sword— the Hydra's eyes grew deep and deeper; the double image of Heracles seemed to whirl away into their depths—then the sword flashed. The head fell and the Lernian Hydra was dead.

Hastily, and with eyes averted, Heracles and Iolaus buried the Hydra's head under a stone. This done, Heracles dipped a pair of arrows into the black blood that was steadily soaking into the ground. These arrows he marked with notches; the smallest scratch from them would procure certain death. They were to be used only in the last extremity. Lastly, Heracles dragged the huge, flabby corpse of the Hydra back to the swamp where he and Iolaus watched it sink under the slow folds of slime from which it had emerged. By way of an ironic tribute, Heracles cast the pieces of the broken crab onto the mirror-smooth surface of the swamp— to mark the place where the Hydra lay. For a few moments they floated, glinting like tattered stars; then they sank and the swamp forgot them.

Iolaus felt Heracles' hand on his shoulder. He glanced up into his hero's face, which was ruddy and shining in the firelight. How was it possible that he'd ever feared this man?

"Come, Iolaus."

Iolaus nodded; and then, taking with them two of the severed heads as evidence of what had been done, he and Heracles made their way among the glowing trees like two weary souls finding their way out of hell.

The Lernian Hydra was only the second of the Twelve Labors. There seemed no end to the deeds Eurystheus set Heracles to do. One, the most degrading, was to clean the Augean Stables, piled high with the manure of untold cattle, uncleaned for untold years. Another time, Heracles took the sky from the shoulders of the Titan Atlas, and had to trick the dimwitted giant into reshouldering the burden. Finally, Eurystheus conceived one last labor: Heracles must go down to Hades and bring back the dreadful three-headed hound Cerberus.

Even so, the Labors were accomplished; even then, there was no peace for Heracles, until at last he was taken to Olympus to be made a god. Before that, there was one other deed: by command of Zeus, Heracles journeyed to the distant crag where great Prometheus had been chained in anguish through long generations. It was Heracles, whose father was Zeus and whose mother one of the people of Prometheus, who freed the Titan from his punishment. Through the deeds of Heracles, Zeus had learned to accept that the race of mortals would endure.

Windigo

BY HERBERT T. SCHWARZ

Windigos were cannibal spirits feared by the Ojibwa and Cree peoples. This Ojibwa story describes how the windigo came into existence.

O n the northern shores of Lake Nipigon there once lived an Indian trapper by the name of Windigo.

There came a particularly cruel winter, cruel both for Windigo and for all the living creatures around him. It was so cold that the air crackled and the game vanished. Windigo had to go further and further from his cabin in search of food, and he became hungrier and hungrier as he tracked wearily back each day empty-handed.

Eventually, for his mere subsistence, he was forced to drink a brew made from the bark of a tree. When even this was depleted, he was weak, hungry, cold, and crazed with fear. In desperation, he prayed to an evil spirit for help.

His call was not unanswered. He had a dream, and in his dream an evil spirit promised to help him by bestowing supernatural powers on him.

When Windigo awoke from his dream, he saw that it was a clear, cold night with a full moon. He was still suffering biting pangs of hunger, but he was suddenly no longer weak or tired.

With enormous swift strides he walked south and soon approached a distant Ojibwa village. His eyes blazed as he gave three blood-curdling yells, which so terrified all the Ojibwas in the village that they fell down in a faint. No sooner had they fainted than they were all turned into beavers by Windigo's evil sorcery.

At last Windigo had enough food to eat, so he began to devour the beavers one by one. As he was eating them, he began to grow taller and taller; first as tall as a wigwam, then bigger than the trees, then taller than the highest mountains, until his head was high above the clouds. The bigger he grew, the hungrier he became. So, when he had eaten all the beavers in the village, Windigo went away in search of more food.

Meanwhile, Big Goose had been away hunting in the forest and did not know that his village had been destroyed by Windigo. As he was returning from the hunt, he was surprised not to see smoke rising from the campfires, and when he came nearer, he found his whole village in ruins and all its inhabitants gone.

At first he thought that a war party of some unfriendly tribe must have carried off all his friends. But when he saw the huge footprints of Windigo in the snow, he realized that something very strange had taken place. As brave as he was, he knew he could never defeat such a monstrous giant.

So Big Goose sat on the ground feeling very afraid and unhappy, and he prayed to the Great Manitou for help.

Suddenly he was startled by a noise close behind him. Then there emerged from the bushes a great Bear Medicine Man, carrying a very large medicine bag. The Bear Medicine Man put his arms around Big Goose and blew his supernatural powers into him. Immediately, Big Goose grew and grew until he became a huge and mighty giant called Missahba.

With giant strides, Missahba caught up with Windigo near Hudson Bay, and there they had a violent fight, hurling great rocks, mountains, and glaciers at each other. All across the land, people trembled in their wigwams as the earth quaked around them. After two weeks Missahba killed Windigo, and the evil spell was broken.

Big Goose shrank from his giant size and became once more an ordinary Ojibwa. And all the beavers devoured by Windigo were set free and again assumed their human form. The arduous journey home from Hudson Bay took them many months, but they were all very happy to reach their village once more.

MONSTERS AND MONSTER KILLERS

Theseus and the Minotaur

BY GAVIN O'RAHILLY

Theseus was another of the great heroes of the Greeks.

I. The Voyage to Crete

Although his mother was a princess, Theseus grew up without a father. One day his mother took him outside the city, to a place where a great boulder lay on the earth. "On the day that you can lift this rock, I will tell you who your father is," she said.

The day came when Theseus could lift the huge rock. Below he found a sword and pair of sandals, which he brought to his mother. "They were put there by Aegeus, King of Athens," she told him. "Take them to him, and call him father. Yet know that the god Poseidon has come to me in dreams, so you may call him father, too."

After saying goodbye to his mother, Theseus set out for Athens. He wanted to emulate his boyhood hero, Heracles, so he took the difficult coast road, which ran through lands ruled by giants and brutal outlaws. Theseus defeated them one after the other, so that he arrived in Athens with the reputation of a hero.

Aegeus was overjoyed to see his son, but Athens was in mourning. It was time for the tribute that the city owed to Minos King of Crete—young people, seven men and seven women, to be fed to the dreadful Minotaur, a monster half-bull and half-man that lived in the centre of the Cretan Labyrinth.

Theseus insisted on joining the victims, so he could fight the monster. As the black-sailed ship weighed anchor, Aegeus cried out that each day he would look for his son. If some god spared his life on Crete, the returning ship was to hoist a white sail, so that the king could know the good news from afar.

→ Slowly, the bright-eyed ship pulled out onto the rolling sea, the sailors straining at their oars until a steady breeze came up, and the sunlit headlands fell behind.

Standing at the ship's prow, Theseus offered up a prayer to his divine father. "Oh great Poseidon, lord of the dark sea and the dark places under the earth where the bright sun never looks, if you are indeed my father give me victory in the darkness of the Labyrinth." So he prayed to great Poseidon, and the god sent up dolphins from the depths to play around the ship as darkness fell.

On they sailed to Crete, to the harbor city where King Minos ruled. Terrace after terrace of white-walled houses rose up the hills, to heights roofed over with bright gold. On the broad-planked wharves the armored soldiers of the king were waiting, to lead the hero and his companions through the streets. With cries and weeping, the Cretans crowding round threw flowers at the young people doomed to die.

Theseus and his followers were led along a pathway upswept with cypresses, until past the pillars of the palace gates a rank of women greeted them. One above all stood out: a girl in her first womanhood, full of grace and swiftness, clad in simple white. As she looked upon the captives, Theseus met her eyes, until she blushed and looked away. Some god made him call out "Hail, princess!" and drop upon one knee, before the guards led them into the palace where grim Minos sat. The arms of his gold throne were shaped like dolphins, and Theseus smiled at the omen.

"Why is it that you smile, you whom the gods have already given up to death?" said Minos.

"Because, oh king, I know the deathless gods give victory to those they wish to honor," Theseus replied.

Minos gave the slight suggestion of a nod. "As great Zeus is my father, why will the gods honor you, manling?"

"Because Poseidon the Earthshaker is my father, and he has sent me here to sacrifice this dark thing you keep underground." As Theseus said this, there was a stir about the throne, and the priestess he had hailed slipped through the guards to take her place beside Minos.

"Sister's daughter Ariadne," said the king, "Whom do you name first to go to meet the Dweller in the Labyrinth?"

"This one, lord," the princess said, pointing to Theseus. And again she turned her face away.

"So be it," said the king. "Let the others stay under guard, and send this one into the Labyrinth."

II. The Labyrinth

They took Theseus to the temple, to wash him and paint him with strange designs. They gave him rich foods and wines, which he refused to eat, fearing they were drugged; and in the night the priestess Ariadne, sister's daughter of the king, came to him.

"Stranger, who are you?" she whispered when she stood before him.

"My mother named me Theseus. My father is Aegeus, King of Athens, but by my mother's oath I truly am the son of great Poseidon."

Ariadne bowed her head. "Then by the Goddess I serve, you are the one foretold. The oracles said this dark one of the earth could never die, until the gods sent one to kill him." She took his hand a moment.

Then she opened out the bundle hid beneath her mantle and gave Theseus a sword, wrought with patterns and designs on blade and hilt. He held the cold blade a moment close against his forehead.

"This you'll need more," she said, and she gave him a wound ball of woollen twine. "Tie the end upon the door when you go in and let this roll out in front of you. It will lead you to the maze's heart and leave a track for you to follow out, a track you'd never find unaided. For those who enter in the Labyrinth have never yet come out." Theseus took the slight ball in his hand.

"Come," she said, and by the altar fire she lit a torch. Black-hooded priestesses waited at the Labyrinth's bronze-plated door, and silently they swung it back, revealing darkness. On the threshold Ariadne handed him the torch, and behind him swung shut the heavy gate.

In guttering red torchglow Theseus could scarcely see the magic ball of twine as it unwound before him down the steep incline into the earth. Holding the torch low to light the ground before his feet, he started down and ever down into the darkness, gripping his sword.

A few steps into the maze, he could not tell which way led down, or—save for the thread—which way he'd come. Around him pressed the darkness, oppressing him with dread and emptiness, so that he was afraid to go on.

Theseus shook off these thoughts, stilling his mind to listen for the monster's presence. The Minotaur was at home in darkness—it might be waiting on the path ahead of him, might be listening to his footfalls now, might burst upon him from any of the passages that ran ghostly off to either side of the track marked by the dim unrolling thread.

Never level, never straight, the path twisted on. Once bones almost stopped his feet at where the passage narrowed so straitly that he had to wind and stretch his way through sideways; yet in that place the dark cold rock was smoothed, as if by constant passage of some enormous body.

Once past, another long stretch wound down and round, until the wall fell away from his outstretched hand. This unseen cavern must be the earth's womb, at the centre of the Labyrinth. He saw the ball of twine had stopped at last.

All was darkness, and silence, while Theseus listened with all his powers. Was there a sound of something breathing in the dark? At the edge of the dim torchlight a shadowed shape suggested itself, humped like a bull but stretched out like a man. The monster was asleep, betrayed to him by the god, lying on the naked rock beside a bed of bones.

With a cry to great Poseidon, Theseus leapt across the monster's back. He grasped a horn, twisting the grotesque head to one side to expose the throat to his keen blade. The dark shape roared as it tried to rise up under him. Then it sank back, and black blood poured over his hand holding the sword. Giving thanks to the immortal gods, Theseus wiped clean his blade, before he caught up the end of Ariadne's thread and started up again from that place to daylight.

Ariadne was waiting at the door. She washed off from him the monster's blood, and then led him down to where the other young Athenians waited by the black-sailed ship. So they left Crete before King Minos could pursue.

The victorious hero sailed back to Athens, with his companions and his Cretan bride. But Theseus left Ariadne on the island of Naxos, where some say the god Dionysus claimed her as his bride. Theseus continued on to Athens, but whether distracted by mourning for Ariadne or by rejoicing for his homecoming, he forgot to hoist the white sail that would give his father hope of his return. Aegeus saw the black sail from the cliff on which he watched, and despairing that his son was dead, he leapt into the sea. Ever since it has been called the Aegean Sea.

Theseus returned to Athens and ruled as king.

Dedalus and Icarus

The Labyrinth was cut into the earth for Minos by the craftsman Dedalus. So skilful was Dedalus that Minos imprisoned him, to prevent him from ever serving another king. In his captivity, Dedalus studied how the wings of birds were made, so that he and his son Icarus might escape by flight.

The wings were made, and when the day came Dedalus counselled Icarus to fly carefully: not too near the waves, lest they soak his feathers and he drown; nor too high toward the sun, lest it melt the wax that held his feathers. They flew away from Crete, and Dedalus reached the mainland safely. But the young man, intoxicated by the power and beauty of his flight, soared up into the heavens, until the heat loosened his feathers, and he plunged to drown in the sea.

Sketco and the Grizzly Man

BY ROBERT AYRE

"Sketco" is a name for the Raven among the Tahltan peoples of northern British Columbia and the Yukon. This story has been edited for length.

Far spent after many wanderings, the Raven one day staggered into a village, seeking rest and comfort, only to be met by such wailing and lamentation as he had never heard before.

"What grieves you?" he asked one old woman, who sat with her arms crossed, rocking to and fro and weeping. The old woman went on swaying and crying and was not able to answer. "What troubles you?" Sketco asked a younger woman, who was also crouched in misery.

But the young woman could not speak. The Raven asked his question over and over again, with the same result, until a blind old man, hearing his voice, hobbled out and said: "Who comes? I hear a stranger's voice."

"It is Sketco, the Raven. Why is your village in such distress, old man?"

"The men are out hunting and the women sit and weep," said the old man in a quavering voice. "I am old and blind or I would be out hunting, too!" he exclaimed, his weak voice rising as he clenched his skinny hands. "The Grizzly has taken eight of our young boys. And he carries off our young girls. Night after night, he steals into the village, and he never goes away without killing. When our strong attack him, he smashes them to the earth with one blow of his arm and breaks every bone in their bodies." The blind man finished in a groan.

"I will help you," said Sketco. "Give me something to eat, for I have come many miles, tramping and flying, and I am worn out." The old man did not hear him, but two small boys ran and brought him food and drink. He sat down and ate ravenously and then, to the surprise of everyone—the women even stopped weeping in their amazement—rose up and changed his shape and flew off over the village.

At length Sketco found the cave of a huge bear, all ringed round with bones, stinking of blood and death. Sketco called for the beast to come out, and then saw the Grizzly Man was his uncle—who long ago had drowned his brothers in the sea, and tried to drown him too. Sketco was frightened, but so was his uncle. After an awkward pause, the Grizzly Man pretended to be friendly.

"Come into my house," said Grizzly Man amiably, "and let us have a feast together."

"I will not go into your filthy den." The Grizzly looked at Sketco with hatred. "And I do not eat the flesh of men."

The Grizzly smiled, but his smile was worse than his black look of enmity. He shrugged his shoulders and sat down on the ground. "Very well, I must entertain you here, in the sunlight."

"That's better," Sketco said. "But I am hungry. Let us go and get some salmon. I have a harpoon that never misses. The head is made out of a ghost's rib."

The Grizzly Man watched the Raven's movements as he picked up the spear which he had stuck in the ground, and balanced it in his hands as if to strike.

"Come," said Sketco. Grizzly Man rose, and together they went down the hill on the other side, tramping all day and eating berries along the way.

"Your river is far," said the Grizzly suspiciously, time and time again, and Sketco always answered: "The best fish are always far to seek." By nightfall, they heard the roar of the water and at last came to the brink of the canyon through which the river raced. After Sketco had plunged his harpoon into the water several times and brought out three or four gasping, lashing salmon, they went up to an open space above the river and made a fire to cook the catch.

At every move, Sketco watched the Grizzly and the Grizzly watched

Sketco, each fearful of the other. But the Raven was careful to show no sign of weakness, nervous as he was. Once he turned in time to catch his uncle standing over him with a big stone in his hand ready to crush his skull in. When Sketco looked into his eyes, the bear smiled feebly and let the stone drop. Sketco said nothing, but he did not sleep that night.

The Grizzly tried to remain awake, too, fearful of being murdered in his sleep, but weariness overcame him. When he awoke in the morning and found that he was still alive, he began to think that Sketco meant him no harm after all. But the Raven had a scheme in his mind.

"Heap up the fire," he said; "make it blazing hot. I have some cooking to do." While the bear piled branches on the flames, Sketco went about gathering stones. He came back with six, each as large as an apple, and dropped them into the fire.

"What are you doing with the stones?" the Grizzly Man asked curiously.

"Can't you see?" Sketco answered. "I am baking them."

"Baking stones! Why? I never heard of anyone baking stones!"

"You live too much to yourself, up there in your den on the hill," said Sketco, laying another branch across the fire. "You should go about the world as I do, and learn what is going on."

"I go about too much for some people!" The Grizzly laughed coarsely.

"Have you ever visited the land of the dead?" asked Sketco, sitting down by the fire and poling at it with a stick.

"No," said the Grizzly. He looked behind him. "Are we not going to eat?" he asked nervously.

"Oh, yes, in a little while. Did you ever eat stones?" the Raven asked him.

The Grizzly looked at Sketco stupidly. "Do you mean to tell me you are going to eat those hot stones?"

"There is nothing I like better than baked stones," said the Raven. He stirred the fire and with his stick jerked out one of the stones. It was so hot that he could not pick it up in his fingers.

"But one of those would burn a hole through your belly!"

Sketco shrugged. "Did you ever try one?" The astonished bear shook his head. "Then how do you know?" Sketco picked up the stone in two sticks, lifted it to his mouth, and pretended to swallow it. What he really did was toss it on the ground behind him, but he was so skilful that the near-sighted bear man was utterly deceived. He was dumfounded. He could do nothing but sit blinking and gaping.

Sketco smacked his lips and licked the corners of his mouth with his tongue. "Ah!" he sighed. "That is sweet! Will you have one?" He fished out another hot stone and pushed it toward his uncle. But the Grizzly Man wet his finger and touched the stone with the tip of it. He drew back, wincing with pain.

"Did you think it would be cool?" asked the Raven. "It is too hot for the fingers, of course, but the stomach is warm to receive it." He lifted the second stone to his lips and again pretended to gulp it down. "Sweet! Sweet!" he exclaimed. "You must have courage if you are to enjoy the sweet things of this world. I am surprised to see the terrible Grizzly Man is so easily frightened, he who crunches the bones of mighty chiefs and whole villages! Oh, well, if you are afraid to taste the stones, my friend, I shall have to eat them all myself."

The Grizzly Man gulped and blinked. "Are they good for you?" he asked.

"They give you strength." The Raven clenched his fist and crooked his elbow. "Do you see that muscle? Is that bad for a young man?"

"I am getting old," mumbled the bear.

"Then you should eat baked stones for breakfast. They will keep you young and lusty. I shall never grow old."

"I am feeling rather hungry," the bear admitted reluctantly.

"It is foolish to be hungry when there are plenty of baked stones for the eating. They will only be going bad," said Sketco. "I can never eat more than three at one meal." He raked another stone out of the fire. "This one is a bit scorched, but that adds to the flavor."

"I ... perhaps ... I think I might try one ... a small one ... not too hot," said the Grizzly uncertainly.

"I wouldn't persuade you against your will," said the cunning Raven, pretending to swallow the third stone and speaking with his tongue in his cheek as if his mouth were full.

"Please give me one," said the Grizzly, who now had a great deal of respect for the Raven and was much milder in his manners.

"The third was the best of all," said Sketco. "The longer they cook, the better they taste."

"Get me one out!" demanded the bear, a little more gruffly.

"As you will." Sketco pulled another stone out of the fire and lifted it on the two sticks. "Shut your eyes and open your mouth."

The Grizzly Man opened his mouth wide and shut his eyes. He flinched as he felt the heat of the stone on his face, but he kept his head back and his jaws open.

"Wider," said the Raven. The bear stretched his mouth open still wider. Sketco dropped the hot stone in.

The Grizzly Man gulped and screamed as it tumbled down his gullet into his stomach. His eyes watered, and he danced up and down with the frightful pain, holding his belly with both hands. Louder and louder he yelled, squirming and jumping, and, throwing himself on the ground, he writhed and rolled in agony.

"This is your punishment," said Sketco coldly, looking down at him. "You will never again murder people and devour them. You will never again drown innocent boys in the sea."

The Grizzly sprang at him, growling and foaming at the mouth, but Sketco stepped back and the bear fell headlong into the fire, which was not burning low. He pulled himself out and began running to the river, but before he had taken three steps he pitched over and fell dead on the ground.

"That is the end of you and all your evil," said the Raven, looking down at his body.

Sketco looked at the Grizzly and thought of the little boys murdered, so long ago, and of the village, laid waste by the monster's greed and wickedness .... Then he changed into his Raven shape and soared above the tree-tops. As he sailed over the village, he could see that it was beginning to stir. Freed of the Grizzly's tyranny, the people who were left were beginning to make a new life for themselves. Sketco remembered that they had asked him to be their Chief, just as the Shark People had wanted him to stay with them and lead them; but he rose higher on his broad black wings and vanished into the North, content to be remembered in their tales.

Kyrilo the Tanner

BY IDA ZEITLIN

This myth is told like a fairy tale.

In the glorious city of Kiev, more years ago than the hairs of thy head, Vladímir the Prince ruled on his throne, and for his golden heart was named Little Brother to the Sun. And he had one daughter, so beautiful and kind that, to him upon whom her glance fell, it was as though he had received a silver ruble.

And the years followed swiftly one upon the other, until an evil chance befell Vladímir the Prince and the city of Kiev. From a deep cavern in the mountainside, beyond the city walls, a devouring dragon came forth upon the highways, and his nostrils belched black columns of smoke and his eyes spat venom and tongues of flame issued from his mouth. And he stretched himself before the city gate so that none, either afoot or on horse, might enter or go forth, and he called for the flesh of a maiden to gorge his hunger. And the lamentations of the people rose toward heaven, and the knights of Vladímir the Prince buckled on their armor and did battle with the monster. Yet to none was the victory given, but the earth was strewn with the bodies of the slain.

And at length the lots were cast and a maiden went forth to the city gate, and the dragon seized her and bore her to his cavern, and peace descended upon the people of Kiev but terror dwelt in their hearts. And in the fullness of time the dragon again issued forth from his cavern and called for the flesh of a maiden to gorge his hunger, and again the lots were cast and a maiden went forth. And whether the lot fell upon peasant or noble, upon soldier or merchant, he must needs yield his daughter up to the jaws of the dragon, and many maidens went forth to his summons but none returned. And all the people of Kiev were bound together in the bitter brotherhood of sorrow.

And so it came to pass that the lot fell upon the palace of Vladímir the Prince. And he cried: "I will not suffer thee to go, my daughter. But I myself will battle with the dragon and slay him, or perish at his hands."

But the maiden answered: "Nay, little father, this may not be, but where the hazard falls, there let it lie. Be of good cheer. Who knows but that this monster will have compassion on me and spare my life?"

And she bade farewell to Vladímir the Prince, and went forth alone to the city gate where the dragon awaited her coming. Yet she could not choose but weep, and the sound of wailing arose from the streets and walls of the city, and Vladímir the Prince walked apart and knew himself not for suffering. But the dragon heeded naught, and seized the maiden in his arms and bore her away to his foul cavern in the mountainside.

And when he looked upon her, he saw that her beauty was such that it cannot be dreamed or pictured but only told in a tale, and he grew faint with love of her and embraced her, saying: "Thou art too fair to perish, little dove. Thou shalt abide with me and keep my house. Thou shalt feed my hunger and slake my thirst and comfort my weariness. And I will bring thee bright jewels from the bowels of the mountains, and soft raiment from the marts of the East. And I will guard thee as I guard mine eyes."

And each morning ere the dragon departed to spread havoc over all the land, he plucked huge trees from out of the earth and tore great boulders from the mountainside, and rolled them before the mouth of the cavern to be his sentinels. And when he returned at nightfall, he removed them and entered in, and ate of the food which the Princess had made ready and lay down at her feet and slept.

And it chanced one day that the Princess sat alone, and meditated upon the bright city of Kiev and upon the palace of Vladímir the Prince, and she heard a sound as of the barking of an animal, and through the crevices between the branches and the boulders that sealed the cavern's mouth, her little dog came creeping. And when he beheld the face of his mistress, he leaped upon her and barked without let or pause, and would not be quieted. And she fondled him in her bosom and her tears bedewed his head.

And presently she bethought herself, and took a charred twig and wrote therewith on a fragment of white birch-bark, and with a golden hair from her head she bound the birch-bark to the neck of her little dog. And pointing the way toward the palace of Vladímir the Prince, she whispered in his ear: "Be thou my courier, little friend, to bear these tidings to the Prince, my father, and ease his heart that is bowed down with care. And bring me in return some word of comfort for the dark hours of my captivity."

And the little dog did not cease from barking, but went forth from the cavern and ran to the palace of Vladímir the Prince. And the Prince saw the fragment of white birch-bark bound with the hair of his daughter, and read thereon the words: "Little father, I am in life and health, but the dragon holds me captive. Jewels from the heart of the mountain hath he laid at my feet and treasures from the deeps of the sea. Yet to live with a dragon is to live with sorrow. May God have thee in his keeping."

And the Prince wept with joy that his daughter lived, and with sorrow that the dragon held her captive. And he bound a letter to the neck of the little dog, and wrote therein: "Be of good courage, my belovèd child, and with God's help I will deliver thee."

And the little dog returned to the cavern, and crept through the crevices between the branches and the boulders that sealed its mouth, and when the Princess read the words of her father her spirit was at peace. And so each day the little dog went to and fro as a courier between the palace and the cavern. And the prince pondered upon his daughter's plight, and sought how she might be delivered from the bonds of the dragon.

And after many days of deep thought, he wrote to her, saying: "Thou must try if thou canst win from the dragon by thy woman's wit the name of him whose strength will prevail against his strength."

And when the dragon returned at nightfall the Princess placed rich food before him and sweet wines, and when he had eaten and drunk she played to him upon a harp of gold and he laid his head in her lap and was content.

And she smiled softly upon him and caressed him with her white hands and said: "Thou art dauntless of heart, my friend, and mighty of sinew, and there is none can name himself thy peer. Yet dost thou walk in constant peril at the hands of thine enemies, and my heart is fearful lest harm befall thee. For if thou shouldst be slain, what cruel fate were mine!"

And the dragon, listening, smiled an evil smile and answered: "Be not fearful, little dove, for there is no arm so strong that it will crush me nor no sword so keen that it will pierce me through. These are but idle fancies, fit for a beldame's mumbling."

"In truth, my lord, I know not what they be, but only that they weigh upon my soul and rob me of my peace. Tell me, I pray thee, is there no man in all the world to match thee, arm for arm and strength for strength?"

And the brow of the dragon darkened in wrath and he cried: "What are these things to thee? Nay, if it please thee, question till the dawn. Thou shalt learn naught of me."

"Thou dost not well to chide me, my belovèd, nor to conceal from me thy secret thoughts. I prithee, speak, and ease me of my burden. Is there in all the world no man to challenge thee?" And she clasped her white arms about his neck and entreated him so piteously, that all his strength forsook him and he yielded to her will.

"In all the world there is one man who is my single peer. His strength is as the strength of ten, for he walks in the light of God. Still have I naught to fear from him, for he is a simple man and knoweth not the might of his right arm. Yet if it came to pass that I should seize his daughter, then it might be that he would learn his strength and rend me limb from limb. He dwells within the walls of Kiev and his name is called Kyrilo, tanner of hides. And now, enough of these things. I have flown today from the snow-crowned peaks of the North to the fair valleys of Arabia. I have seen strange sights and wrought strange deeds, and I am spent with weariness. Play thou upon thy golden harp, and I will sleep."

And in the morning the dragon bade the Princess farewell, and plucked huge trees from out of the earth and tore great boulders from the mountainside, and rolled them before the mouth of the cavern to be his sentinels. And presently the little dog crept through the crevices between the branches and the boulders, and the Princess bound to his neck a letter, wherein she had written: "Seek out Kyrilo the peasant, the tanner of hides, who dwells within the walls of the city of Kiev, for he only shall prevail against the dragon."

And so the little dog ran to the palace, barking all the way, and the

Prince read what his daughter had written and his joy knew no bounds. And he dispatched couriers to every corner of the city to find out the house of Kyrilo the Tanner, and he ordered his coach to be brought, that he might be borne to the house of Kyrilo, and do honor to him that was appointed of God to slay the dragon.

And Kyrilo stood at a huge vat, wherein he plunged at once the skins of a hundred bulls, and when he saw that the Prince approached him and smiled upon him as upon his friend, his great hands trembled and the hundred skins were rent in twain as though they had been wafers.

And the Prince said: "I greet thee, Kyrilo the Tanner, appointed of God to slay the dragon that lays siege to our city and destroys our children. And I pray that thou go forth against him as speedily as may be, to rid us of his presence and to deliver the Princess, my daughter, from captivity."

But Kyrilo gazed in dismay upon the Prince and answered: "Thou art deceived, my lord. I am a peasant and a tanner of hides. I ply my craft from dawn to dark, and have no skill in aught that lies beyond. How should I strive against this monster? I would not anger thee, but fight I cannot!"

"Nay, thou must venture, Tanner, for only thou canst win the victory. The dragon hath declared it."

But Kyrilo would not, and still he shook his head and made reply: "Thy pardon, Prince. My task is to tan hides. I cannot fight."

And at length the Prince in sore distress left the house of Kyrilo, and returned to the palace and gathered his knights and his councillors about him and said: "The head of this peasant is as thick as his arm is mighty. How should he be moved to this combat?"

And the oldest and sagest of the councillors arose and spoke. "Sire, if thou think it good, send to the tanner five thousand young maids of the city of Kiev; let them go from the hut of the peasant and from the palace of the noble, and let them kneel before him and plead with him, for the sake of their lives that are doomed, to do battle with the dragon. Though his head be thick, yet his heart is gentle, and it may be that he will heed their prayers."

And the children went forth from hut and palace to the house of Kyrilo the Tanner, and they knelt before him and cried: "Pity us, Father Kyrilo, pity us! Go forth against the dragon and vanquish him! Else will he devour us each one in turn, while yet the sweets of life remain untried. Go forth and slay him, Father Kyrilo! Thou art our savior and our hope. We will not leave thee, but kneel here at thy feet till thou hast pledged thy word to fight the dragon."

And they clasped their hands and wept, and the youngest wept more bitterly than all the rest.

And in the end Kyrilo yielded to their prayers and said: "Go with the Lord and weep no more, for your tears afflict my soul. I will do battle with the dragon and slay him by God's grace, or stick in his throat till he perish for lack of breath."

And so he prepared to go forth and meet the dragon. And he called for hemp to the measure of three hundred *poods* [about five tonnes], wherewith he fashioned a stout rope and bound it about his body. And with his knife he hewed a great tree down and took it for a cudgel in his hand. And so he went to the cavern in the mountainside.

And he lifted his voice and summoned the dragon from his hiding-place, crying: "Come forth, vile monster and skulker in the dark! It is Kyrilo the Tanner who calls. Come forth and match thyself against me, arm for arm and strength for strength!"

And the dragon hissed and snorted and gnashed his teeth in fury, crying: "What midge is this that buzzes in the field? Do thou but bide my coming, and I will bolt thee at a single gulp!"

"Then tarry not, but come! Here is the open field, fit meeting ground for warriors, and here an enemy who summons thee to combat. Wilt thou come forth, or is thy spirit faint as thy soul is cursed?"

"Thou braggart fool, thine hour is near at hand. I will seize thee by thy yellow hair, and thy soul shall swoon for terror and thy bones rattle in their sockets! I will dash thee into fragments against the mountainside and leave no remnant save a single hair, whereby thy mother may know thee for her son."

"All things by the will of God, and a truce to words! Come forth, thou unclean spirit, or I will enter in and pluck thee by the tail!"

And the dragon crawled forth from the cavern, hissing and snorting in a very frenzy of rage, so that the mountains echoed and the earth rocked with his clamor. And his nostrils belched black columns of smoke, and tongues of flame issued from his mouth.

And when Kyrilo looked upon his evil countenance, he was seized with a great bitterness, and his strength was as the strength of a hundred. And he rushed upon the dragon and there in the open field they clashed, breast to breast, and a ring of fire compassed them round about. And Kyrilo belabored him with his mighty cudgel and smote him hip and thigh, until the dragon prayed for quarter and sank prostrate at the feet of his enemy.

And Kyrilo swung his cudgel above his head and would have brought it down upon the head of his adversary, but the dragon cried: "Stay, Kyrilushka! Why wouldst thou slaughter me and all my seed? When have I injured thee or wished thee ill? Rather should we dwell together in peace and brotherhood, for thou and I, my friend, might share the earth and none arise to challenge our dominion. We will divide the land in equal parts, and on this side I will hold sway and on the other thou, and half of all the treasure of the world shall be thy share and half shall come to me. And if our rule should profit others naught, how can it injure us?"

And God lent to Kyrilo the serpent's guile, and he answered: "Let it be so. And for a mark between thy lands and mine, let us plow a furrow in the earth, and what lies on the one hand shall be thine and on the other, mine. And thou shalt draw the plow!"

And Kyrilo fashioned a plow of metal so heavy that a hundred oxen could not move it. And he yoked the dragon to the plow, and with his flail of iron he goaded him. And the dragon drew the plow from Kiev to the sea and made a furrow twenty fathoms deep. And when they came to the sea, his head hung low between his shoulders and his strength was as the strength of a babe, and he cried: "Release me from the yoke, Kyrilushka, for we have cleft the earth in twain."

And Kyrilo answered: "As we have cleft the earth, so let us cleave the waters. Or one day thou wilt come and cry with a loud voice: 'Thou has stolen my water, Kyrilushka.'"

And Kyrilo drove the dragon into the blue sea, and the waters covered him and the plow drew him down through the depths to the nethermost cave of the ocean, and there he lies even now and the plow of Kyrilo the Tanner lies on his back.

But as for Kyrilo, he returned to the cavern, and with one arm he flung aside the boulders and with the other the branches, and he bore the Princess to the palace of her father, and the people came forth to welcome him and made merry in the streets of Kiev.

And Vladímir the Prince said to Kyrilo: "What is there in my gift that thou wouldst have? I will heap thy vats with gold to the brim and running over. I will name thee my friend, and seat thee at my table and serve thee with bread and salt and pay thee homage."

And Kyrilo, the mighty warrior, made answer to the Prince: "For thy love and fair speech God will reward thee. But if my vats are filled with gold, where shall I wash my hides? And if a peasant sit at a prince's table, who shall know him for a peasant? Nor did I fight this fight for thee, my lord, but to dry the tears of children."

And Kyrilo returned to his house, and he fought no more battles but washed his hides and dwelt in the grace of God.

And it is told that in the midst of the steppes the mountain of earth, upturned by the dragon when he drew the plough from Kiev to the sea, still rises twenty fathoms to the sky. And the peasants till the soil on either hand, but the mountain of earth shall rise forever to the glory of the name of Kyrilo the peasant, the tanner of hides.

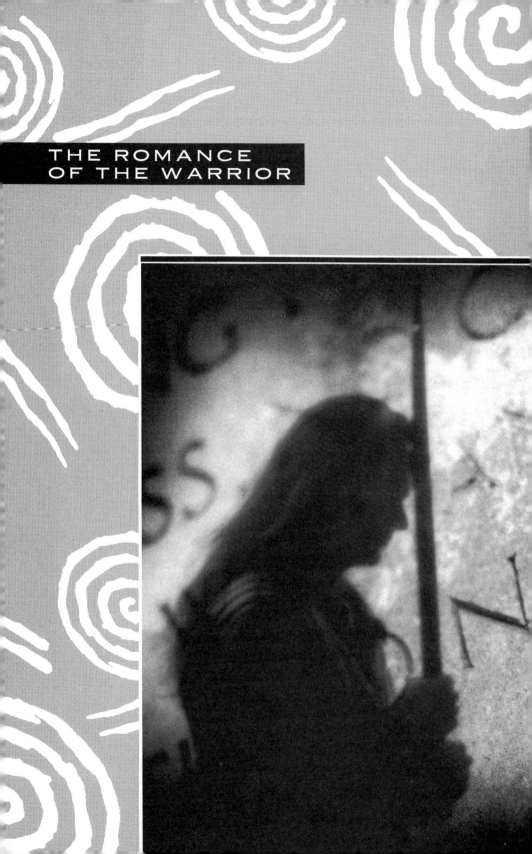

THE ROMANCE
OF THE WARRIOR

Throughout history the figure of the warrior has been surrounded by an aura of tragedy and beauty. People dream of being heroes, and often that has meant being a hero in war.

Since warriors are most often men, and young men, it has usually fallen to women to love the glamor that surrounds them. The story of the young woman who rejects the old king to love a young man of her own choosing is one of the most important in western literature. Or is it that young women dream of being warriors themselves?

What does it mean to be a warrior? The dreadful machinery of modern war has made a warrior's courage almost unimportant, and has robbed war of all its romance. But is the warrior just someone who fights in battle, a soldier with brute weapons? Or is the warrior anyone who fights for justice and truth, who defends the powerless and gives a voice to those who cannot speak? If we reject the figure of the warrior, we deny that life is full of strife.

The Trojan War

BY ALFRED J. CHURCH
AND OTHERS

"Achilles and the Death of Hector" (Part IV) by Alfred J. Church, edited by Kathleen Lines. Other narrative by Sean Armstrong.

The warriors who fought at Troy have been famous ever since the poet Homer wrote their story in The Iliad, *almost 3000 years ago.*

I. The Judgment of Paris

The Trojan War, which ended in such misery for so many people, began as a quarrel among the gods. There was a wedding, between the sea-goddess Thetis and a mortal prince, to which all the gods and goddesses came. When the merriment was at its height, hateful Strife, sister of War, appeared among the guests.

"You gave me no invitation," she cried, "but here I am. This is my gift—a present to whoever is the fairest of you all!" She threw a golden apple among the goddesses before she vanished. The goddesses Hera, Athena, and Aphrodite each thought the apple properly belonged to her. No one, not even Zeus, would dare award it to one above the others.

Clever Hermes suggested a solution. Near the city of Troy, which Zeus loved above all other cities in the world, there lived a shepherd named Paris. One of the sons of the king of Troy, he was famous both for his beauty and his judgment. Why not command him to choose among the goddesses?

So one day, as Paris was tending sheep up in the hills and thinking thoughts about beautiful women, Hermes appeared with the golden apple, and gave him the command of Zeus. The young man rolled the apple reflectively on his hand's palm, as the three goddesses appeared before him. Each, as she passed before him, promised something to make him choose her. Athena promised wisdom and undying fame, and Hera said she'd make him lord of all Asia; but Aphrodite smiled at him and stroked her finger across his lips while she promised him the love of the most beautiful woman in the world. So Paris gave her the apple. *Gave apple to Aphrodite*

The most beautiful woman in the world was Helen. All the princes of Greece had came to court her, until her father—or rather her stepfather, for great Zeus was in fact her father—feared that if he gave her to one suitor he would earn the others' enmity. He made them all swear to support whichever one he chose, and then he gave her to Menelaus, King of Sparta and brother to Agamemnon, the High King of all Greece.

Not long after Helen and Menelaus were married, Aphrodite sent Paris to Sparta, in fulfilment of her promise. Paris saw Helen and loved her; and she loved him. She agreed to elope with him back to Troy. So powerful was the enchantment Aphrodite wove surrounding Helen that all the Trojans, from old King Priam down, swore they would never let her go back to the Greeks, even when Agamemnon and Menelaus sent an embassy requesting her return.

So war was inevitable. Now when Paris won Aphrodite's promise, he also won the hatred of Hera and Athena. Both were goddesses most powerful in war, and both now were deadly enemies to Troy. Henceforth the gods would intervene, until virtually all had chosen sides for Troy or the Greeks. *War between Greece and Troy*

II. The Anger of Achilles

The outraged brothers Menelaus and Agamemnon sent to all the princes who had sworn to uphold the marriage of Helen, reminding them of their oath. And so a vast force of ships—tradition says a thousand ships, with about thirty warriors per ship—assembled on the sheltered beach at Aulis, not far from Athens. Not everyone came willingly—Odysseus, the king of the small western island of Ithaca, newly married with a baby son, thought war in far-off Asia a catastrophe.

Others came avid for renown, like Achilles, the son who had been born to Thetis. Destined to be the greatest warrior in the world, he had already grown miraculously to manhood. When he was a baby, his mother sought to make him invulnerable by dipping him into the Styx, the river of the underworld. The black waters touched him everywhere, except on the heel by which she held him. It was here that he was destined to get his death wound, in the spot we still call the Achilles tendon.

After some difficulties the Greeks set sail, landing on the far shore of the Aegean by the walls of Troy. They gaped at the massive towers and the gilded roofs: here was a city that seemed almost to belong to the gods. The Trojans gazed out in dismay at the western barbarians who had come to war on them. The Greeks pulled their ships up on the beach in lines and made a camp beside them, waiting for the Trojans to come out and fight. The Trojans withdrew behind their high walls, and waited for the Greeks to lose heart, or for hunger and disease to weaken them. So it went through nine hopeless years of war.

Certain of the Greeks, led by Achilles and the wily Odysseus, raided up and down the coast of Asia Minor, seizing cattle, treasure, and captives to sell as slaves. Among their captives were young women, and it was over the possession of these women that Achilles quarreled with Agamemnon.

When the captives were shared out, the girl given to Agamemnon was the daughter of a priest of Apollo. Her father called on the god for help, and Apollo shot arrows of plague into the Greek camp, until the smoke of burning pyres hung in the air. The Greek lords held a council, and the oracles told Agamemnon that the only way to stop the plague was to hand the girl back to her father. In a foul temper, the king agreed, but swore he needed compensation. In fact, he needed the girl who had been given to Achilles. Achilles jumped to his feet and offered to kill Agamemnon then and there; then he stormed out of the meeting, swearing that from now on, he and his men would refuse to fight, no matter how desperately the Greeks needed them.

Achilles then called upon his divine mother Thetis, asking her to plead with Zeus to send disaster to the Greeks. Zeus agreed—he was fond of Thetis, and he favored the Trojans anyway, although his wife Hera and daughter Athena supported the Greeks. That night, he sent a lying dream to tell Agamemnon to attack Troy the next day. Believing the false dream promised victory, Agamemnon formed up the Greeks for battle—all save Achilles and his men. The Trojans, when they saw the Greeks advance, put on their armor and prepared to fight as well.

III. Hector and Andromache

Priam King of Troy had many sons; but greatest of all was lordly Hector. On this day he stood forth before the Trojan lords and bade them arm themselves for battle. The massive doors of the pillared Scaean Gate were opened, and the Trojans poured forth onto the plain before the city.

After he had dressed for battle, Hector went to find his young wife Andromache, for they were newly married and had a baby son. He found her walking on the high city walls, carrying the boy so he might see his father go out to battle. The baby boy they called Astyanax, Little City Prince, because his father saved the city from the fury of the Greeks; and he was a lively and loving child. When she saw strong Hector in his armor, Andromache's heart failed her, and she spoke thus to him:

"My lord, you have been fortunate in battle and some god has protected you so that you won great honor. But I fear that one day the god's protection may forsake you, or some other god will hate you, and the merciless bronze will pierce your flesh and let out your life's blood, so that your face will lie against the dust and your soul fly down to gloomy Hades. That day I shall be a widow; yes, and more than a widow. For pitiless Achilles slew my father and all my seven brothers, so my mother died in her insensate grief; you are not only husband to me, but father and mother to me as well, and brother also. If you should die, my lord, think then how our boy will suffer, having no father to protect him. When he is older, and seeks to contest in games, or comes to take a place at table when the meat is roasted and the wine is mixed and poured, the other boys will push him rudely down, saying 'Let him hide his face, for he has no father in this world.'

"My lord, have pity on me, and stay this day upon the wall, where you can see the tide of bloody battle, and lead the men of Troy with shouts and wise direction. For from this place you can see all the lords of the Greeks, and penetrate their stratagems."

"Alas, my dearest heart," said Hector. "These things I cannot do. You know that I must lead the Trojan lords. I could not bear that they should think I was a coward. Full well I know that the immortal gods have destined Troy for destruction, yet for a moment we prevent it. But it is not

for Troy I fear, but for you my princess, when I think how the Greek lords will beat you with their spear butts and lead you captive into a strange land, there to waste your lovely cheeks in barren tears and bitter labor."

He reached then to take his little son in his arms, but the boy was frightened by the grim helmet with its nodding horsehair plumes, and hid his face against his mother's shoulder. Both his parents smiled then, and Hector took off the helmet so his own face was revealed, and kissed the boy to make him laugh. He lifted him up in his great manly hands, and prayed to live to see the day the boy was counted greater than himself. This prayer the gods refused to hear.

Then Hector and Andromache said farewell, and she turned back into the city with her women, fearing she would never hear his voice again. But Hector went down to fight against the Greeks, and ever he was foremost in the battle.

The fighting ebbed and swayed across the Trojan plain, and many men fell in agony to the dust, while their spirits started down the stony path to Hades. Zeus had decreed the Trojans should that day have victory, and none could withstand Lord Hector. The greatest champions of the Greeks were carried wounded out of battle, until at last the Greeks were driven back to where their beached ships lay, while the Trojans still stormed forward and sought to set the ships on fire.

And all the time great Achilles waited in inaction, his troops beside him idle, to let Agamemnon most bitterly regret the dishonor he had done him. But when the first ship began to burn, his bosom friend Patroclus besought him, saying, "Great Achilles, desperate is the condition of the Greek lords, and if no help comes to them I fear there will be no later day for them to bethink the wrong they did you. Let me put on your armor, and lead your men, the peerless Myrmidons, to battle, so that all may think great Achilles has come to fight, giving hope to the Greeks and confusion to the Trojans." Achilles looked at Patroclus, dearest to him of all men that walked the earth, and gave him leave.

So Patroclus led the Myrmidons into battle, and drove the weary Trojans back with deadly spearplay. Then the god Apollo breathed new strength into Hector so that he came to meet Patroclus. When the two heroes faced each other, Patroclus stumbled, and Hector killed him. The Greeks and Trojans fought long over his body and the glorious armor of

Achilles, until at last the Trojans stripped off the shining armor and gave it to Lord Hector. The Greeks fled before the Trojans to their ships, and the fighting ended for that day.

The Greeks sent heralds to Achilles, to say his bosom friend Patroclus was dead. Achilles threw himself upon the ground, pouring handfuls of the dust upon his head. His divine mother Thetis came to him to ease his anguish. "Rest, my son," she said, "and I shall ask the god Hephaestus to make new armor for you, armor fitting for a god. For I know that after you have slain Prince Hector, you will not live long."

While Achilles lay wracked with grief within his tent, the council of the Greeks, led by wise Odysseus, advised Agamemnon to make up their quarrel. So he did, with full apologies and lavish gifts, and Achilles accepted them. "I have no joy now," he told the heralds, "but to see the death of him who killed my friend, and to weary myself with killing Trojans."

Dawn came. Food was served from great cauldrons to the men who were waiting to kill each other that day. Great Hector put on the armor of Achilles, taken from Patroclus, while across the plain Achilles took the new armor made for him by Hephaestus . . . .

IV. Achilles and the Death of Hector
by Alfred J. Church. Edited by Kathleen Lines.

Meanwhile the Greeks made ready for battle, and in the midst Achilles armed himself. He put the lordly greaves about his legs, and fitted the corselet on his breast. From his shoulders he hung the sword, and he took the great shield that Hephaestus had made, and it blazed as it were the sun in heaven. Also he put the helmet on his head, and the plumes waved all around. Then he made a trial of the arms, and they fitted him well, and bore him up like wings. Last he drew from its case his father's spear, which Chiron cut on the top of Pelion, to be the death of many, and none might wield it but Achilles' self. Then he spake to his horses: "Take heed, Bayard and Piebald, that ye save your master today, nor leave him dead on the field, as ye left Patroclus."

Then Hera gave the horse Bayard a voice, so that he spake: "Surely we will serve thee, great Achilles: yet for all that, doom is near to thee, nor are we the cause, but the gods and mastering Fate. Nor was it of us that

Patroclus died, but Apollo slew him and gave the glory to Hector. So shalt thou, too, die by the hands of a god and of a mortal man."

And Achilles said: "What need to tell me of my doom? Right well I know it. Yet will I not cease till I have made the Trojans weary of battle." Then he shouted to his Myrmidons and drove forward into battle, eager above all things to meet with Hector and to slay him.

Now Zeus had inspired the hearts of both the Greeks and the men of Troy to hurl themselves into battle. And as the combat waxed furiously there arose a dreadful strife among the gods by reason of the division between them (some being for one side and some for the other). With a great crash they came together so that the earth shook and the heavens rang as with a trumpet and Zeus heard the noise of their conflict from where he sat on high Olympus. Among those who supported the Greeks this day were Hera, Poseidon, Hermes, and Athena; but Apollo and Artemis, the river god Xanthus, and Ares and Aphrodite helped the men of Troy.

In the midst of the battle Apollo snatched Hector from the sight of Achilles and bade him keep from the forefront of the battle. But many were the heroes that fell before Achilles, for he fought savagely and without mercy. And, although often impeded in his vengeance by the intervention of Apollo and other gods, yet sustained by Hera, Poseidon, and Athena he ceased not to pursue and slay the men of Troy. So great was his onslaught that the forces of Troy parted before him, and wheeling he turned and drove them before him across the plain towards the city.

King Priam stood in a tower on the wall and sore troubled was he when he saw the progress of the battle. He hastened down to the guardians of the gates and said, "Keep the wicket-gates open that the troops may enter in, for they fly before Achilles." And men hastened in, wearied with toil and thirst, and covered with dust, and they flocked into the city, nor did they stay to ask who was safe and who was dead, in such haste and fear did they flee. Only Hector remained outside the walls, standing in front of the Scaean Gate.

And Priam, from the wall, saw Achilles coming swift as a racehorse across the plain, his armor glittering bright as the brightest of the stars. And the old man groaned aloud, and cried to his son Hector, where he stood before the gates, eager to do battle with this dread warrior:

"Wait not for this man, dear son, wait not for him, lest thou die beneath his hand, for indeed he is the stronger. Of many brave sons has he

already bereaved me. Come within the walls, dear child; come to save the sons and daughters of Troy; come in pity for me, thy father, for whom, in my old age, an evil fate is in store, to see sons slain with the sword, and daughters carried into captivity, and babes dashed upon the ground."

Thus old Priam spake, but could not turn the heart of his son. And from the walls on the other side of the gate his mother called to him, weeping sore, and said:

"Come within the walls; wait not for this man, nor stand in battle against him. If he slay thee, nor I, nor thy father, nor thy wife, shall pay thee the last honors of the dead, but far away, by the ships of the Greeks, the dogs and vultures will devour thee."

So father and mother besought their son, but all in vain. Hector was still minded to abide the coming of Achilles.

And Achilles came near, brandishing over his right shoulder the great Pelian spear, and the flash of his arms was as the flame of fire, or as the rising sun. Then Hector trembled when he saw him, nor dared to abide his coming. Fast he fled from the gates, and fast Achilles pursued him, as a hawk, fastest of all the birds in the air, pursues a dove upon the mountains. Past the watchtower they ran, past the wind-blown fig tree, along the wagon-road which went about the walls, and they came to the fair-flowing fountain where from two springs rises the stream of eddying Scamander. Past the springs they ran, one flying, the other pursuing; brave was he that fled, braver he that pursued; it was no sheep for sacrifice or shield of ox-hide for which they ran, but for the life of Hector, the tamer of horses. Thrice they ran round the city, and all the gods looked on.

And Zeus said: "This is a piteous sight that I behold. My heart is grieved for Hector—Hector, who has ever worshipped me with sacrifice, for now the great Achilles is pursuing him round the walls of Troy. Come, ye gods, let us take counsel together. Shall we save him from death, or let him fall beneath the hand of Achilles?"

Then Athena said: "What is this that thou sayest, great sire?—to rescue a man whom Fate has appointed to die? Do it, if it be thy will; but we, the other gods, approve it not."

Zeus answered her: "My heart is loath; yet be it as thou wilt."

Then Athena came down in haste from the top of Olympus, and still Hector fled and Achilles pursued, just as a dog pursues a fawn upon the hills. And ever Hector made for the gates, or to get shelter beneath the towers, if haply those that stood upon them might defend him with their spears; and ever Achilles would get before him, and drive him towards the plain. So they ran, one making for the city, and the other driving him to the plain.

But as for Hector, Apollo even yet helped him, and gave him strength and nimble knees, else could he not have held out against Achilles, who was swiftest of foot among the sons of men.

When the two came in their running for the fourth time to the springs of Scamander, Zeus held out the great balance of doom, and in one scale he put the fate of Achilles, and in the other the fate of Hector; and lo! the scale of Hector sank down to the realms of death. And then Apollo left him.

Athena lighted down from the air close to Achilles and said: "This, great Achilles, is our day of glory, for we shall slay Hector, mighty warrior though he be. For it is his doom to die, and not Apollo's self shall save him."

Then the two chiefs came close to each other, and Achilles threw the mighty spear, but Hector saw it coming and avoided it, crouching to the ground, so that the spear flew above his head and fixed itself in the earth. But Athena snatched it from the ground and gave it back to Achilles, Hector not perceiving.

Then Hector threw his long-shafted spear. True aim he took, for the spear struck the very middle of Achilles' shield. It struck, but pierced it not, but bounded far away, for the shield was not of mortal make. And Hector stood dismayed, for he had not another spear. He knew that his end was come, and he said to himself: "Now have the gods called me to my doom. Zeus and Apollo are with me no more; but if I must die, let me at least die in such a deed as men of aftertime may hear of."

So he spake, and drew the mighty sword that hung by his side: then as an eagle rushes through the clouds to pounce on a leveret [a young rabbit] or a lamb, he rushed on the great Achilles. But he dealt never a blow; for Achilles charged to meet him, his shield before his breast, his helmet bent forward as he ran, with the long plumes streaming behind, and the gleam of his spear-point was as the gleam of the evening star, which is the fairest of all the stars in heaven. One moment he thought where he should drive it home, for the armor which Hector had won from Patroclus guarded him well; but one spot there was, where by the collarbone the neck joins the shoulder (and nowhere is the stroke of sword or spear more deadly). There he drove in the spear, and the point stood out behind the neck, and Hector fell in the dust.

Then Achilles cried aloud: "Hector, thou thoughtest in the day when thou didst spoil Patroclus of his arms that thou wouldst be safe from vengeance, taking, forsooth, no account of me. And lo! thou art fallen before me, and now the dogs and vultures shall devour thee, but to him all the Greeks shall give due burial."

But Hector, growing faint, spake to him: "Nay, great Achilles, by thy life, and by thy knees, and by thy parents dear, I pray thee, let not the dogs of the Greeks devour me. Take rather the ransom, gold and bronze, that my father and mother shall pay thee, and let the sons and daughters of Troy give me burial rites."

But Achilles scowled at him, and cried: "Dog, seek not to entreat me! I could mince that flesh of thine and devour it raw, such grief hast thou brought me. No ransom, though it were ten times told, should buy thee back; no, not though Priam should offer thy weight in gold."

Then Hector, who was now at the point to die, spake to him: "I know thee well, what manner of man thou art, that the heart in thy breast is iron only. Only beware lest some vengeance from the gods come upon thee in the day when Paris and Apollo shall slay thee, for all thy valor, by the Scaean Gate."

So speaking he died. But Achilles said, "Die, hound. My fate I meet when Zeus and the other gods decree."

Then he drew his spear out of the corpse, and stripped off the arms; and all the Greeks came about the dead man, marvelling at his stature and beauty, and no man came but wounded the dead corpse. And one would say to another, "Surely this Hector is less dreadful now than in the day when he would burn our ships with fire."

Then Achilles devised a ruthless thing in his heart. He pierced the ankle-bones of Hector, and so bound the body with thongs of ox-hide to the chariot, letting the head drag behind, the head that once was so fair, and now was so disfigured in the dust. So he dragged Hector to the ships.

Achilles did not long survive the death of Hector. Paris shot him with an arrow—Paris shot the arrow, but Apollo guided it so that it struck him in his vulnerable heel; and so he died. After this Paris also died, and Helen was without a husband. The war dragged on without end.

One morning the lookouts on the Trojan heights reported that the Greeks had sailed away, tearing down their camp. The Trojans found the beach deserted, save for a giant wooden horse and one lost Greek, who said the horse was an offering to Athena.

The Trojans debated what to do with it. Some were saying to burn it, when the Greek captive said the horse had been made huge so the Trojans would never take it within their city walls to their own temple of Athena. So the Trojans decided to do just that. This was what the Greeks—who had left the man behind—had counted on.

One voice predicted fire and death if they brought the horse within the walls, but no one listened. It was the princess Cassandra, daughter to Priam and Queen Hecabe. Apollo had desired her, and given her the gift of prophecy to win her love; but when she still refused it, he added the curse that no one ever would believe her visions.

Then the Trojans gave themselves over, high and low, to joy and celebration of the ending of the war.

In the still night, when all of Troy lay in a happy drunken sleep, armed Greeks climbed out from their hiding place in the horse's belly. They opened the city gates to let in the main Greek army, which had landed in the darkness while the Trojans drank and danced.

The streets flickered with new fires and echoed horridly with screams and groans. Odysseus and Menelaus ran to the house where Helen was. She knelt before Menelaus, and her unchanged beauty overthrew him. He forgot all the years between, and raised her up to embrace her and forgive her.

It did not go so well with others in the city. The men were killed as they struggled to awaken, and left lying where their deaths took them. The women were driven captive through the streets with the butts of spears. The city burned as the sack went on for days, until the drunken Greeks assembled on the beach outside the ruined city to divide the spoils.

The women were shared out. Queen Hecabe, who had lost all her children, shrieked curses at the Greeks. The beauty of Princess Cassandra, which had aroused Apollo, aroused King Agamemnon also, so he took her to his ship, along with heaps of rich spoil to adorn his palace in far-off Mycenae. Andromache, Hector's widow, they gave to one of the cruellest of the Greeks; and they threw the boy Astyanax from the towers of the city wall, for the Greeks feared him if he grew to manhood.

Then the Greeks turned home, after quarreling among themselves. They sailed by different routes, and soon great Zeus the Thunderer—who had loved Troy above all other cities—struck them with a storm that scattered all their ships, and ruined many. Others were blown far off course, among them Odysseus, whose troubles on the homecoming become the subject of *The Odyssey*.

The War Trail of Sin'opa

BY FRANCES FRASER

The figure of the warrior is surrounded by an ancient glamor, but are only men dazzled by that glamour?

To "count coup" is to tell public stories among the warriors.

She was the daughter of the war chief Oma-kis'kena. They say the old chief was disappointed because his first-born child was not a son, though later he had sons among other children. But she was the oldest child of his first-chosen wife, and it may be that he loved her a little more for that. So during his lifetime he taught her the hunting skills, the war craft he would have taught the son he wished she had been. The other men watched her interest in these things with amused indulgence, and if sometimes they thought her training was not quite what a girl should have, they did not say so to Oma-kis'kena. Her mother and the other wives kept the lodge and cared for the family, teaching the women's lore to younger daughters and performing with patient drudgery their endless tasks.

Then, when she was sixteen years old, a bad sickness ran through the camps of the Siksika [the Blackfoot], and when it abated Oma-kis'kena and his wives were among those dead.

Relatives offered homes to the younger children. A husband, they said, would be found for the girl, for she was old enough to marry. But she had other plans. She refused the offers of homes for the children. The offers of marriage she declined often with such insults as to ensure that would never be repeated.

"I will have my own lodge!" she said. "I can hunt, and better than most men. My sisters and my old grandmother will do the women's work. We will look after ourselves!"

And so they did. The rest of the tribe looked on, admiring the independence of the family and finding unobtrusive ways to help and protect.

She was a good hunter. Their lodge was well kept. Things went well. But day by day her resentment of her sex grew and deepened in bitterness. Many things added to it—the restrictions placed on girls of marriageable age, the women's rites she was compelled to take part in, the far more interesting ceremonies she was excluded from, the placid acceptance of their inferior status by the other women, and, most of all, the overtures from the men of the tribe—for they say she was little, and lovely, and there was no man who did not want her.

She envied the war parties above all things. As she watched the young men making their sacrifices in the Sun Dance, she thought how gladly, how bravely, she would make the vow and submit to the torture. When the coups—the brave deeds—were counted around the fires, no ear listened more readily, there was no voice quicker in praise than hers.

At last a day came when she could no longer remain passive. When the fires burned low that night and the women and the children were gone to the teepees, the men talked of war and raids, and they planned a raid. In the dark shadows, unseen and unsuspected, they had a listener, who heard, and smiled, and went to prepare for a journey.

All the next day, the camp buzzed as the war party prepared for their raid. Women stitched extra moccasins, packed bags of food. Arrowheads were chipped and fitted, bows were tested. The medicine man, MoKi'wa, burned sweetgrass on a little fire, and made his search for signs and portents. The signs were good, he told them, and the girl, listening, took his words for a sign to herself.

In the dark before moonrise they left, and she went with them, walking in silence, concealed by the night. When the moon rose, she dropped behind, so they would not notice her. An hour before dawn the warriors slept, and when they awakened, she was with them.

They brought her to the chief. Surrounded by the older warriors, men who had ridden with her father, he stood eying her coldly. She held her head erect, and met his angry look squarely. A little admiration for her crept into his unwilling mind. But no Blackfoot maiden had ever so conducted herself, and had it not been for the memory of her father, she would have been dealt with harshly indeed.

Threats and persuasions alike were unavailing. She would not go back to camp. "My father taught me to be a warrior," she said. "I will come with you, or I will come alone."

Support for her came from the medicine man. "I read the signs for the raid," he said, "and the signs were good. Send her away, and you may send our luck with her."

"When has *our* luck come from a woman?" scoffed the chief. But he listened and consented. The warriors went on their way.

Through quiet valleys, over darkening hills, the warriors walked. Then, far ahead, they saw the campfires, and they smiled grimly. As softly as night itself, they were moving now. A twig snapped, and they held their breath. An owl hooted, a small animal rattled through the underbrush, and their hearts beat faster. If they were discovered they would die, and their dying would neither be quick nor easy.

Shadows under a cloudy moon they stood, just outside the camp. In barely breathed whispers the chief deployed his men. "Let me go first," said the girl. The chief shook his head, but a sign from the medicine man changed his mind, and she disappeared.

The warriors waited, expecting every minute to hear the outcry which meant discovery. Then, out of the darkness, she reappeared, leading two fine horses. She tethered them, and went back for more, the men with her. Six horses she took from the enemy camp, and when a sentry stirred she killed him, quickly and quietly, and came to the meeting place.

When the party returned to the Blackfoot camp, she came in triumph. Standing by the council fire, the chief spoke to his men. "The daughter of Oma-kis'kena has proved that she is a warrior." His voice rang over the camp, and the tribesmen hurried to the spot. "What reward shall we give this warrior?"

The answer came back, "Give her a man's name!"

It was not what the chief intended, but he turned to the girl and asked, "Do you want that, a man's name?"

"That, and my coup!" she answered.

The chief turned to his men. "Sin'opa has gone on to the Sand Hills," he said. "Shall we give *his* name to her?"

"Yes," shouted the warriors.

"And what else?" said the chief.

"I want my coup," said Sin'opa.

The chief turned to his warriors. "Does Sin'opa count coup with *us*?" he shouted.

The answer came back, "Yes!"

The sound of the drums came up like thunder out of the mountains, and the high rolling chant of the coup songs shook the trees by the river.

From that time on, she rode with the warriors, led a man's life. She wore men's clothing while on raids and hunting, but in the camp she dressed as the women dressed. She was little, and very lovely, the Old Ones say, and the men she rode with thought of her often, not always as the warrior she was. And the women hated her.

As she grew older, she counted many a coup of horses and other trophies, many a scalp. In the camp she was silent and withdrawn, knowing well the hostility of the women. But on the trail with the warriors she was happy, and by the fires there was laughter and camaraderie, though no man dared to touch her. In battle she was savage; to the weak or cowardly she was cruel, but for a wounded or a dying warrior her hands were gentle and her voice was kind. The men she rode with came to believe that where she led, they could not be defeated.

When she was in her twentieth year they made her a war chief. In the lodges of the Ku'tenai, the At'sina, and the Pesik'na ta'pi, men shivered when her name was mentioned.

Then a night came, a raid on the Ku'tenai. The alarm was given. Someone tripped? A horse neighed? It doesn't matter now. The warriors of the Ku'tenai poured out of their lodges, and our men fled. When they gathered again, Sin'opa was not with them.

The Siksika went back into the camp like a hailstorm. They killed every Ku'tenai, warrior or not, who stood in their path. The poles from the lodges fed the fires, and by that light they searched for and found their chief, dying. They lifted her gently, and brought her out. She was dead before morning.

They brought her body home, all the long way to the Blackfoot camps, the scalps they had taken from the Ku'tenai tied to her dead hands. She sat by the council fire, dead, and they counted her coup for her, counted the scalps she held in her hands as part of it. They counted all her coups, one last time.

They put her body in her own teepee, with all her trophies, her weapons, her men's clothing. The tribe moved away, and they left her there.

But after a while, her own warriors, the men she had ridden with, came back. In the lodge beside her body they put women's clothing, the tools women use, the trinkets women love, even a tiny moss-bag for a baby, for the thought had come to them that maybe, in the Sand Hills, she would be content to be a woman, and it might be that she might want to do these things.

Deirdre and the Sons of Uisnach

BY DAVID GUARD

The story of Deirdre [pronounced DEER-dree or DARE-drah] and the sons of Uisnach [u-WISH-nach, the "ch" being pronounced as in "loch"] is perhaps the best known of the Irish myths. One of "The Three Sorrows of Storytelling," it describes the tragedy of the rebellious Deirdre and her love for Naisi [NEE-sha], a young warrior of the Red Branch.

I. The Lovers

Deirdre was born during the autumn festival, when her father was entertaining the court of King Conor [*CON-nor*] of Ulster. The festivities stopped when the wild, piercing cry of the newborn child was heard. The druid who was present prophesied the child would grow up so beautiful and strong that men would fight and die over her, bringing civil war into the land. Her name, he said, would be "Deirdre," which means "the troubler" or "the bringer of strife."

The warriors said the child should be put to death, but Conor was already intrigued. He ruled instead that she would be brought up in isolation from the world, in the company of old foster parents and the poetess Levarcham [*Le-VAR-ham*]. She would see no other people, and when she was old enough he himself would marry her. This way the prophecy would be prevented.

In her fifteenth year, when Levarcham told the king that Deirdre grew fairer and fairer so that even the wild creatures of the woods rejoiced in her, he announced to his household that when the time of the first greening was over, when the wild rose runs like a flame through the land, he would have Deirdre for his bride and consort. On hearing of this, Deirdre was overcome with sadness. She lost all desire for food; her sleep was restless and filled with visions. To Levarcham it seemed her very spirit had deserted her as she spent her days of melancholy sitting by the window listlessly embroidering a cloth. Each earlier twilight brought a colder wind. All too soon the snows came back from the north and settled upon the forest.

One cold bright morning, her foster father was skinning a calf on the snow outside to cook for dinner. While she looked, a raven came gliding over the snow to the slain calf and began drinking its bright blood. "I think," said Deirdre, "that the man I marry will have those three colors about him: his hair black like the raven's, his face as fair as the snow, with cheeks as red as that blood. I saw such a young man in my dream last night, but I know not where he is, nor whether he exists at all."

"I am amazed you should be telling me your dream in just this way," said Levarcham, "for down in Emhain Macha [*Evan MAH-hah*, where Conor's fort was] they use those very words in praise of a young champion who is living there. He is among Conor's knights, and his name is Naisi, of the three sons of Uisnach. You shall have the loyalty and protection of this knight when you are the wife of his king. Come away from your dreaming and turn your thoughts to the happiness which is in store for you."

"The king is so old," said Deirdre, "and my dream is more real to me than anything you say about the king."

"The king is a great man," said Levarcham. "He is very kind and has given you everything. At the beginning, he saved your very life!"

"Oh mother," cried Deirdre, "if you want me to go on living, go to Naisi of my dream and ask him to come and find me in the forest outside the wall."

"Child, you cannot know the danger in what you ask. If your foster parents hear of it, they are bound to tell the king."

Deirdre made no answer, but remained sad and silent throughout the last winter of her childhood, her eyes often filling with tears at the memory of her dream. Levarcham grieved for her. She worried that Deirdre's heart would break if she and Naisi were not allowed to meet, and she feared Conor's furious vengeance if such a thing were discovered. After many fretful days, because she loved Deirdre more than anything in the world she made her difficult way down to the encampment at Emhain Macha to seek out the three warrior sons of Uisnach. There she found them engaged in feats and contests on the green in front of the palace. She was not disappointed with Naisi, for he was the most beautiful of the brothers, with the colors of the girl's dream indeed upon him. Putting aside her worst fears for their safety, Levarcham told him of the young girl and her dreams.

"Deirdre! I remember that name from some tale of my childhood," said Naisi.

"Then come soon and hunt deer in the solitudes north of the forest," said Levarcham, "and there in some glen or on the hillside you may find her and none will know of it. Such wilderness is open to the flight of the owl as well as the soaring hawk."

So it was told. Levarcham and Naisi parted with a wave, and she made her journey back to Deirdre. Late the next day, Levarcham and Deirdre ventured outside the wall as they often did, to wander the lonely hillside and collect herbs and flowers. The forest was warm with the new life of spring.

"There is a strange thing," Deirdre said, "for just now I heard the cry of the jay, but it was the one he gives in alder month, at the nesting time. And now listen! That was the bark of the hill fox, but it was the one he gives in his own mating season, many months ago!"

"Hush," said Levarcham, "and look!"

They saw three young men coming up the glen together, and Deirdre looked at them in wonder. As they drew nearer she knew they were the sons of Uisnach, and this was Naisi, the tallest and handsomest of the three. The brothers passed by without turning their eyes at all toward the watching women. They were singing as they went and their song was pure enchantment to Deirdre and Levarcham, but at the same time the shadows were lengthening in the wood and the sons of Uisnach were widening the distance between them. Deirdre hugged Levarcham hurriedly, gathered her skirts, and ran after them.

Naisi left the chase of the deer and turned to make his way through the green glooms of the royal forest. In a clearing under a high ceiling of branches, Deirdre slipped out near him in passing, pretending not to notice him.

"Oh, that is a fine heifer going by," Naisi laughed.

"And why not?" said Deirdre. "The heifers just keep growing where there are no bulls."

"But you have the bull of the province all to yourself," said Naisi. "I have heard he loves you as some old miser loves the dragon stone he hides among the cobwebs near the roof."

"All of that is true," she said. "It was against the wishes of the king that I've come out of my house without my mother. I have spent all my life behind the wall of the dreary fortress where he has me locked away. At the new moon they are coming to take me down to his palace. The bird will be freed from the fowler's net only to be forced into the wicker cage. Forgive me for speaking this way, Naisi, but I would love you as in days of old, when Dectera the queen loved the green harper, and went away with him and was seen no more by her own people."

"Ah but you couldn't, Deirdre! Have you forgotten the druid's prophecy?"

"Are you rejecting me then?"

"That I am," said Naisi.

She rushed at him and caught him by the ears. "Two ears of shame and mockery if you don't take me with you!"

"Woman, leave me alone!" cried Naisi helplessly, laughing and going round and round with her.

"You will do it," she said. "You must!"

Prying loose her hands and taking them firmly in his own he said, "Now surely, Deirdre, there is no burly warrior of the Red Branch can match your courage, but it may be that you speak so freely from knowing so little of what might happen."

"What bold words from the proud son of a proud family!" she said scornfully.

Naisi tried to hide a smile. She looked at him as though seeing him for the first time, and before more could be said, she put her mouth on his and with the confusion that went through them, a blaze of red fire came upon her in an instant, and just as quickly faded away. Naisi had never held a woman so beautiful in his life, and from that moment he gave to Deirdre the love he never gave to another living thing. He stepped away from her a little and spoke to her evenly.

"There is still time, Deirdre. For your own sake will you go back to your house and stay there until the king calls for you?"

Looking at him steadily she said, "I value this one perfect day with you, Naisi, more than a lifetime with Conor." Then she smiled brightly and slipped her arm in his, saying, "Besides, we're young, and that's the time to see the world. We can always come back!"

They hurried down the wooded slope first walking, then running, in search of his brothers. Before long they came to the friendly hounds who led them to the clearing where the brothers were hunting. Ainlle [*ANN-lah*] and Ardan greeted Deirdre and made her welcome, but they said, "There will be trouble because of this. Is she not the girl who is fated to destroy Ulster? However, we'll not be disgraced as long as we stay together. There is not a king in Erin [Ireland] who would not make us welcome."

With all speed they summoned those of their following who were under the sword-bond to put together food and clothing, and they went away that night, with three times fifty men, three times fifty women and the same of grayhounds and menials, with Deirdre in their midst, mingling with the rest. Thus it was, the Clanna Uisnach deserted the house of Conor macNessa, going over the border into exile.

So Deirdre went with Naisi and his brothers to Alba, the islands and hills of western Scotland. There they lived for six contented years. The three sons of Uisnach hunted game in the highlands and fished in the clear lochs. Deirdre sometimes joined them in their hunts, or spent the days making medicines from wild herbs. During the long summer nights Deirdre and Naisi passed the time in conversation and storytelling, or playing chess and making music. They were in every way happy, living free as lords of their own island.

II. The Return

But back in Ulster King Conor never forgot. Never would he forgive for the shame he had suffered. Yet, as time passed and news came back from Alba, people said it was too bad that Ulster should be deprived of three of its bravest warriors because of the passions of the king. Conor considered what they said, and at last agreed. He sent Fergus macRoigh [*MacROY*], one of the greatest of his warriors and most honorable of men, to take a message to the exiles telling them he granted them full pardon and that he wished them to return to Ulster.

Fergus swore he would go to bring the sons of Uisnach to Conor, and that once they landed in Ulster they would stop for nothing until they ate at the king's table. They would come under his personal protection, an oath that bound himself, his sons, and his clan to them. Then he sailed to Alba, finally dragging his ship's keel onto the beach of the island where Deirdre and the sons of Uisnach were.

Fergus sent up his mighty hunting call in the harbor. At this moment the sons of Uisnach were some distance from their fortress, out of sight and almost beyond earshot. The three brothers had put up wicker hunting booths in the forest near the shoreline. In the last booth Deirdre and Naisi had a chess board between them and were advancing the men upon it. Naisi could hear the sound of Fergus's call coming through the shoreline trees, and said, "That is a call we used to hear in Erin."

"It is not," said Deirdre. "It was the cry of a man of these waters."

Fergus gave another mighty roar, and Naisi said, "Again! That is an Irish shout!"

"Indeed it was not," she said. "Let's go on playing. The moment I gain advantage, you begin to welcome distractions! Give me my chance at this game!"

But when a third call was heard, nearer than ever, Naisi leapt to his feet. "Now that was Fergus!" And he sent Ardan running down to the water's edge to welcome the voyagers.

"It may be that Conor is dead," said Naisi.

Then Deirdre confessed that she had known from the first shout that it was Fergus. "I had a vision in a dream last night," she said. "Three ravens came flying to us over the sea from Emhain Macha, and they brought three drops of honey in their beaks. These honey drops they left with us, and took away with them three drops of blood."

"What meaning do you give your dream?" asked Naisi.

"It means Fergus comes to us from Conor with honey-sweet offers of peace. The three drops of blood are Ainlle and Ardan and yourself, whom Conor would flatter and lure into his trap."

As Ardan ran out upon the beach he quickly recognized Fergus and his two sons. These were friends from earliest boyhood, and he cried out to them in affectionate welcome and gave them three kisses. He brought them to the lodges where Naisi and Deirdre and Ainlle gave them another warm welcome, and asked them news of Erin and of Ulster.

"The best news," said Fergus, "is that King Conor is preparing a great banquet for his friends and kinsmen throughout Erin, and he has vowed by the earth beneath him, by the sky above, and by the power of the sun that he will not have a night of rest nor a day of peace until the children of Uisnach return to the land of their home and the country of their inheritance. I have come over as a guarantee for your safety, to see you honorably restored to your places in the Red Branch. Surely it is good to end a feud and put away the sword and spear."

"And surely Conor macNessa forgets," said Deirdre, "that Naisi is now overlord of a land larger than all of Ulster. The world's turned upside down when the king of an island goes as the forgiven guest of the lord of a rock."

"Ah, but one's own country is better loved than any other," said Fergus. "Life is sad when a man wakes in the morning and finds himself too long away from home."

"That is truth to me," said Naisi. "Erin still owns my heart, even though we have made a good life here."

"Deirdre," Naisi said, "in my flight I have brought with me many whose true wish is to see home again, while you are a fixed star by my side, no matter where we go. Many a maiden sighs for the clansman who may never return. There is also the heavy burden of disgrace upon our name, because I fled and did not face the king. Shall I swear to keep my comrades in exile, and let the shame of cowardice rest on the head of their clan?"

"We are of two lands," said Ardan, "still we look upon ourself as of the Red Branch first and foremost."

"It is harmless for you to go with me," said Fergus.

Fergus gave his vow in the presence of his weapons that if any attempt be made upon the lives of the children of Uisnach, he and his sons would leave no guilty head on its shoulders. And Naisi and his brothers in turn agreed that they would not eat food in Erin until they had eaten from Conor's table first.

The decision to return to Ulster was made without Deirdre's consent, and as they wore away that night she shed tears and related dreams and omens, giving Naisi little rest. He said to her, "When we give or take a word, we pledge more than our own one life, but the lives of our clansmen as well. None would be alive today were there not this means of putting away past grievances."

When Deirdre arose next morning, she walked down to the edge of

the water and there saw Naisi and Fergus in a galley together, each preparing to man an oar. Many of their people also were there, stowing their belongings and settling into the ships. She knew they would not be persuaded to stay, so she climbed the steep plank and took a place at the rail on a pile of skins and robes.

All day and into evening, wind and the work of the rowing men brought them steadily southwestward across the cold expanse of the Moyle. Falling far behind them was Loch Etive of the storms, the land of the fresh forest trees. Deirdre took her harp and sat back among the deerskins in the stern of the galley and began to sing a sorrowful farewell to Alba. Then the hands of all the mariners were relaxed and every oar suspended, for the sadness of her song pierced the starry night and dissolved every heart.

III. The Fate of Deirdre and the Sons of Uisnach

The moment they landed on the Ulster coast, a man met them, demanding Fergus come to a feast he had prepared. He had been sent by Conor, who well knew that as a warrior Fergus must observe his own personal *geasa*, or taboo. It was Fergus's *geasa* to never refuse a feast.

Yet the sons of Uisnach had already sworn to stop for nothing on their journey to Conor at Emain Macha. So, without Fergus, but with only his sons Buinne [*BUE-inny*] and Illan [*ILL-ann*], they went on. Deirdre knew that treachery was inevitable, but Naisi would not turn back: that would be to show fear, and a warrior might not show fear.

At Emain Macha, they were not shown to the King's hall, but to the Warrior's hall, the Inn of the Red Branch. Feasting in his own hall, surrounded by warriors who were loyal to him alone, Conor was wracked by conflicting feelings. He sent Levarcham down to the Red Branch to bring word of how Deirdre looked now. Levarcham, frantic to protect Deirdre, came back to tell him Deirdre's years of exile had made her old before her time. This soothed the king, and he went back to drinking. But in a few minutes he was gripped again by rage and jealousy. He sent someone else to report on Deirdre—this time a man named Trendorn, a hereditary enemy of Clanna Uisnach.

Reluctantly Trendorn left the flickering torchlight of the banquet hall and went outside into the darkness. He moved in a stealthy circle around the Inn of the Red Branch, only to find its heavy oak doors barred and its windows shuttered. It would not be easy to approach the sons of Uisnach when they were in such a suspicious mood, Trendorn thought. But at length he discovered a narrow window giving light, climbed up to it from an unyoked chariot which stood near, and peered in to find Deirdre and Naisi playing at chess. Deirdre chanced to look up at that moment and, following his wife's glance, Naisi caught sight of the face at the window. With the spiked and barbed chessman in his hand, Naisi made a fearful successful cast so that it broke the eye in the young man's head. Trendorn dropped down in pain and rage, and ran straightaway to the king to tell him, "I have just seen the loveliest woman in all the world. If it weren't for this unlucky wound I would be there looking at her still!"

Conor sprang to his feet, a flame of fury in his eyes, and threw back his head in loud and cruel laughter. At this, everyone in the palace knew the king's madness was upon him, the blood-thirst once again upon his sword. "Comrades!" shouted Conor, "the truth stands out at last. It is now clear that the sons of Uisnach have come here not in peace, but to make rebellion. My messenger returns from them gravely wounded. Chieftains of the west, will you come to the aid of the king of Ulster?"

"That we will!" they replied in a drunken roar.

"Then everyone with me! Surround the outlaws in the house of the Red Branch!"

The soldiers came rushing forth in a mighty surge over the lawn of Emhain Macha and set upon the Red Branch, yelling fiercely, brandishing torches and flaming spears. When the sons of Uisnach heard the din they called out through the heavy walls of the lodge, "Who is there outside?"

"It is I, Conor macNessa, king of Ulster, and let the matter be in darkness to you no longer. My fighters are set round in among the trees. If the woman Deirdre is put out through the door the troops will go away."

Illand Fairheaded shouted in reply, "These people are here under pledges of safe conduct sworn to them by my father, Fergus macRoigh!"

"By the laws of my own conscience," replied the king, "it is a greater shame upon yourselves and the sons of Uisnach that my wife is in there with them."

"That is true," said Deirdre quietly, "and Fergus has kept you in a dream, but this night must have awakened you, surely."

"You will soon see," said Buinne, hitching his swordbelt around him, "my father Fergus has not abandoned you, nor have we!"

"Now bring up grappling hooks and scaling ladders," shouted Conor, and he sent men scrambling up the red log walls to break in through the high windows of the fortress. But this proved no difficulty to the defenders within, and the attackers were driven repeatedly from the narrow barred windows and ledges with great loss of life, for those who were not struck directly had their skulls cracked by the fall. All remained safe inside the Red Branch, but there was no time for rest or jubilation.

Next there began the low thunderous clout of a battering ram upon the heavy oak door. In the darkness and confusion Buinne Roughred was able to slip unseen from a window, and he leapt into the midst of the unarmed men working the ram, taking them totally by surprise, scattering their firebrands and torches, killing a dozen at his onrush, confounding the attackers with his mighty shout of doom.

Conor, who could see nothing of the man but the torchlight upon his cloak, called out through the darkness, "Who is there, bringing destruction on my men like this?"

"None other than Buinne the Roughred, the first and foremost of the sons of Fergus macRoigh!" came the triumphant answer.

"Now Buinne," said the king, "there is no quarrel between ourselves. I will give you a good gift if you will leave off: a section of land, a place at my table, and the power of my word when it's needed. What do you say to that, Buinne?"

"Better a king's generosity than the favors of a widow," thought Buinne, and he said, "I'll take that gift!" So that was how he went over to the hand of Conor. And it was a good and fruitful mountain he was given that night, but not long afterwards a blight fell upon it, turning it to moorland—waste and profitless.

Deirdre overheard what had taken place, and with a bitter smile she said to Naisi, "By the moon and stars, Roughred Buinne has turned withershins and is gone over to the hand of the king. Now it makes me wonder if *both* sons of Fergus are nothing but their father's echo."

"Buinne is gone, but he did good work before he went," said Naisi, just as the harsh booming voice of the battering ram took up its earsplitting task anew.

"Too much more of that and they'll soon be in among us," shouted Illand Fairheaded. "I'll not desert your cause so long as I can lift this sword." And Illand leapt out and made a furious round of the Red Branch,

the sparks flying from the edge of his weapon like fiery rain, bringing vicious slaughter upon the hireling troops.

"Call him out," said Conor. "This will be as simple as the other." But Illand Fairheaded was a good son, for he never refused aid to anyone in need and he never accepted so much as a calf from anyone but Fergus.

"I claim the royal right of single combat in the name of Fergus macRoigh. My challenge to the household of Conor macNessa!"

Basely the king called his own son Fiacra to him, saying, "It was on the same night that you and Illand were born, and as he is using his father's weapons, so you will have mine: my shield, Ocean; my dart, Victorious; my gapped spear, Slaughter; and my sword, Gorm Glas, the blue-green. Bear yourself manfully against the son of Fergus. You must surely defeat him, or the Crown of Ulster will fall from our hands. The divine powers in these weapons will protect you."

Searching through the dim thickening darkness, Fiacra found the son of Fergus and they made a red-wounding attack upon each other. Those watching on all sides sent up a sigh of deep despair, while the din and harsh sounds of their struggle echoed round the woods and hills. Soon it was Illand who hard-pressed the son of Conor and sent him sprawling. At that moment, Conall Cearnach [*Con-all CHARE-nach*], chief of the knights of the Red Branch, was approaching Emhain Macha in his chariot. He soon heard the mournful sighing of the crowds and the ringing crash of weapons against Ocean, the king's great shield. Conall steered his chariot through the crowd of onlookers to find the fight. In the dim light he believed Conor himself was in great danger beneath the shield, and from the mighty onslaught of his opponent he saw there was no time to waste. Instantly he plunged his spear between the shoulder blades of the unknown assailant. Mortally wounded, Illand looked up and cried, "Was it you, Conall? Evil work you've done, with the sons of Uisnach under my protection."

"What trick has Conor been playing here?" screamed Conall. "He will not get his own son back alive for this!" And with one side twist of his long sword he lifted the head from Fiacra. Then Conall knelt beside the fading Illand, who called out to the sons of Uisnach to keep faith in Fergus, flung his weapons toward the Red Branch, and died on the soft green lawn of Emhain Macha. In grief and rage Conall swiftly remounted his chariot and drove away from the battlefield at full gallop to report the king's treachery toward Fergus and the brotherhood of the Red Branch.

The sons of Uisnach were now left alone to face the onslaughts of hired soldiers.

"Give me the woman!" called Conor once more. "She will not be harmed. It is enough that the king pardons her and calls her to his table and bed!"

Deirdre looked at Naisi and said softly, "No man and woman have loved better. You were my company when the fires on the hilltops were put out and the stars were our friends only. Do you remember that first night in the woods? We lay on leaves, and looked up when the first gray dawn awoke the birds. You thought that I still slept and, bending down to kiss me on the eyes, found they were open. Bend and kiss me now, for it may be the last before our death."

Hearing no answer from within the hostel, Conor ordered the final attack: "Set the Red Branch in a forest of flames! Should any come out of it, put them to the sword!" A wave of the king's men assaulted the Red Branch, sending great sheets of fire running up its timbers.

"He's destroying his own palace, his own kingdom!" shouted Naisi, as a climbing drift of smoke burst into a scarlet tongue of flame before his eyes.

"Let's out and die, or break away if there is any chance in this darkness," said Deirdre. "We will be roasted here surely as pigeons in an oven."

The sons of Uisnach then made a close firm fence of their shields, putting Deirdre in their midst, and came out and away from the blazing lodge. Slicing a path through a hedge of spears, they gave three great leaps over the ramparts of Emhain Macha, leaving their pursuers far behind. But on the next hillside they were forced to pause in their headlong flight, to lie hidden among the tall ferns while they bound the worst of their wounds.

At this, the king frantically summoned the ancient druid Cathbad [*CAFF-fah*] to him, pleading, "If these three run wild again we will have a civil war to contend with. Stop them, druid, before there is such butchery done here that enemies from all sides will be drawn to Ulster in its weakness. I pledge that I will be no further danger to the sons of Uisnach, but let them only make agreement with me."

"Your destiny is to live a great deal longer," the sad-eyed druid told

Conor. "I have no power to oppose this destiny, but my heart is sore within me from the vision I have of it." Reluctantly Cathbad told the king to have his men build roaring brushwood fires below the hilltop where the sons of Uisnach and Deirdre were standing their ground. And when the crackling flames were hot, the druid cast green hazel branches upon them, bringing forth dark billowing clouds of suffocating smoke. All was blotted from view and no man could rightly see the other, only dim choking figures emerging from the gloom or disappearing into it. And with this cloud the druid worked an enchantment upon the children of Uisnach, for they thought themselves to be engulfed in a sea of thick viscid waves, and they soon cast down their weapons and spread their arms abroad as if to swim. And that is how the sons of Uisnach were overwhelmed, and the mercenaries came and took them without a blow, seizing and binding them, to bring them before Conor.

The king called for the sons of Uisnach to be slain, but none of the Ulstermen would stir. A deep shame was rising in each of them. Eoghan [*Owen*] of Fermanagh was among those who had come to Emhain Macha to make alliance with Conor, with whom his western clansmen long had been at enmity. As a first demonstration of loyalty, it fell upon Eoghan to kill the children of Uisnach while Conor macNessa looked on, guarded by his thirty warriors so that no one might approach him in revenge.

They stood on Emhain Macha's once green lawn, with Cathbad's oily cloud still hanging above them in the early morning air, shrouding the smooth hill so that neither the men guarding the bound brothers nor the women watching from the ramparts could be certain whether it was day or night.

"Kill me first," said Ardan. "Being youngest, I have fewer farewells than my brothers."

"Being youngest you should live the longer. I would be first," said Ainlle.

"You have my sword," said Naisi, "the gift of Mannan son of Lir, and its stroke is swift and clean. Let the three of us be struck by it at once, so that none of us may see his brothers shamed."

It was agreed, and Eoghan handed the sword to his strong man Maine [*MAN-ney*] Redhand, who dealt the single blow, beheading the three sons of Uisnach instantly. And the Ulstermen gave three sorrowful shouts and cried aloud.

Their bodies lay side by side on the ground like three beautiful saplings destroyed by a blasting storm. Deirdre knelt beside them, lamenting and kissing them and showering them with her tears. Before long she was led away and made to stand beside Conor, with Levarcham there to comfort her.

Conor ordered his men to dig a grave, and at its foot they raised a standing stone with the name of Uisnach hewn upon its edge in the language of the trees, and their funeral games were performed. It was at this time the druid cursed Emhain Macha and the bloodline of Conor macNessa to the end of race and time.

When Fergus heard of Conor's treachery, he swore revenge. So began a war that ravaged Ulster, as Fergus went to join the King's enemies, and the prophecy was fulfilled. As for Deirdre, the king kept her by him in his household for a year, and in all that time she never smiled. So at last she died.

The king's men laid Deirdre's body in a separate grave near the palace, but during the night the people of the district took her body to rest in the grave of Naisi and his brothers. Conor learned of this and had his men drive sharpened yew stakes through the corpses of the lovers to keep them apart. But the stakes soon sprouted, and by the turn of the year, two graceful yew trees were growing there side by side. Conor had a firm warning from the druid to leave these trees undisturbed and cease all persecution of the dead. The king went no further in the matter but turned his full attention to the war which was afterwards called the Cattle Raid of Cooley.

So ends the tragedy of the children of exile and the sorrows of Deirdre. "May the air bless her, and water and the wind, the sea, and all the hours of the sun and moon."

The Legend of Iroquois Falls

BY MABEL BURKHOLDER

The fur trade brought fierce war to several North American peoples, for whom access to trade goods and a market for their furs became a matter of survival. Tribes like the Iroquois, who lived in areas depleted of furbearing animals, fought to gain the furs of interior tribes like the Cree. Behind these rivalries was the struggle between French and English for control of the fur trade and the continent.

Here is the story of how a Cree woman defended her people. The Ojibwa have a similar story attached to Kakabeka Falls in northwestern Ontario.

O nce a party of Iroquois attacked and killed a band of Crees in the neighborhood of Iroquois Falls, in northern Ontario. They spent two days in collecting the booty and bundling it up in shape to carry; for the spoils were very great.

All the Cree warriors lay dead on the ground; also most of the women. Many had been tortured, and some scalped. Only one old woman had been saved. She was a noted guide, and without her help the Iroquois warriors feared they would have trouble in getting out of the place with their load of plundered furs.

They asked the old woman about the journey, and she told them the river was very swift, breaking into rapids a little farther on; but that her people had always preferred to shoot the rapids, rather than take the longer way around the portage.

"If you are men and warriors," she said scornfully, "you will prefer shooting the rapids also."

The Iroquois were not lacking in daring, and they were very anxious to show their skill before an enemy who mocked them even in the hour of defeat. They decided to shoot the rapids.

"Better throw off the weight, and let your women carry the bundles by way of the portage," advised the old woman. "Remember the rapids are swift, and with a heavy load you might come to some disaster."

They did not know whether to believe their enemy guide or not. Finally they decided to take her advice; so they let their women walk by the shore and carry the bundles.

"I will also walk with the women," said their guide.

"Ho, ho!" shouted the warriors. "You shall come with us to point out the way. Otherwise we could not be sure whether you spoke truly or not. You might be sending us to destruction. Only by coming along yourself can you prove your good faith."

"Very well," said the old Cree woman quietly, "I will guide you down the river."

She took her place at the head of the fleet of Iroquois canoes. Swiftly they glided through the agitated water. Surely they were approaching no ordinary rapids, for a sullen roar came to their ears, like the noise of a great waterfall.

As they neared the falls the Iroquois saw that they were very high, and that no canoe could go over them in safety. They tried to turn back, but it was too late. Then the old Cree woman rose in her place and mocked them. She told them that this was her revenge for their killing of her people. She did not mind going to her own death, for it was glorious to take with her the warriors of the enemy nation.

As she sang her death song, the canoes glided swiftly to the awful brink of the deep and dangerous waterfall. All went crashing over, and no one in them was ever seen alive again.

Arthur and the Two Swords

BY ROGER LANCELYN GREEN

The tales of King Arthur and the Knights of the Round Table still present us with a clear ideal of honor, loyalty, and courage. There are many heroes in the Arthurian legends—Sir Launcelot, Sir Gawain, and other knights; the wizard Merlin and the enchantress Morgan-le-Fay; the tragic Queen Guinevere—but at the center is King Arthur himself, whose knightly ideals animate all in his court.

The Arthurian tales are thought to have a historical core, surrounded by layers of ancient Celtic myth and then reworked for centuries by the mind of the medieval world. The historical foundation is thought to be the fifth century, when the Britons, the inhabitants of Roman Britain, were fighting desperately against Saxon and Scots invaders.

Arthur was the son of Uther Pendragon, the king who had briefly unified the south against the invaders. Despite this brief period of peace, it was clear that dreadful years of chaos lay ahead, and before King Uther was killed he sent the baby Arthur in care of the wizard Merlin to the Land of Mystery, Avalon. There the baby received three gifts from the powers of mystery: he would be the best of all knights, he would live long, and he would be the greatest king his land would ever know. Merlin then gave Arthur into the care of a good knight, Sir Ector, to raise as his own son. So Arthur grew up, not knowing whose son he was, nor what his destiny would be.

Then the land fell upon days more evil and wretched than any which had gone before. King Uther's knights fought amongst themselves, quarreling as to who should rule; and the invading Saxons, seeing that there was no strong man to lead the Britons against them, conquered more and more of Britain.

Years of strife and misery went by, until the appointed time was at hand. Then Merlin, the good enchanter, came out from the deep, mysterious valleys of North Wales, and passed on his way to London. And so great was his fame that neither Saxon nor Briton dared molest him.

Merlin came to London and spoke with the Archbishop; and a great gathering of knights was called for Christmas Day—so great that all of them could not find a place in the abbey church, so that some were forced to gather in the churchyard.

In the middle of the service, there arose suddenly a murmur of wonder outside the abbey: for there was seen, though no man saw it come, a great square slab of marble-stone in the churchyard, and on the stone an anvil of iron, and set point downwards a great, shining sword of steel thrust deeply into the anvil.

"Stir not till the service be done," commanded the Archbishop when this marvel was made known to him. "But pray the more unto God that we may find a remedy for the sore wounds of our land."

When the service was ended the Archbishop and the lords and knights who had been within the abbey came out to see the wonder of the sword. Round about the anvil they found letters of gold set in the great stone, and the letters read thus:

WHOSO PULLETH OUT THIS SWORD
FROM THIS STONE AND ANVIL
IS THE TRUE-BORN KING
OF ALL BRITAIN.

When they saw this, many and many a man tried to pull out the sword—but not one of them could stir it a hair's breadth.

"He is not here," said the Archbishop. "But doubt not that God will send us our King. Let messengers be sent through all the land to tell what is written on the stone: and upon New Year's Day we will hold a great tournament, and see whether our King is amongst those who come to joust. Until then, I counsel that we appoint ten knights to guard the stone, and set a rich pavilion over it."

All this was done, and upon New Year's Day a great host of knights met together. But none as yet could draw forth the sword out of the stone. Then they went all a little way off, and pitched tents, and held a tournament or sham fight, trying their strength and skill at jousting with long lances of wood, or fighting with broadswords.

It happened that among those who came was the good knight Sir Ector, and his son Kay, who had been made a knight not many months before; and with them came Arthur, Sir Kay's young brother, a youth scarcely sixteen years of age.

Riding to the jousts, Sir Kay found suddenly that he had left his sword in his lodgings, and he asked Arthur to ride back and fetch it for him.

"Certainly I will," said Arthur, who was always ready to do anything for other people, and back he rode to the town. But Sir Kay's mother had locked the door and gone out to see the tournament, so that Arthur could not get into the lodgings at all.

This troubled Arthur very much. "My brother Kay must have a sword," he thought, as he rode slowly back. "It will be a shame and a matter for unkind jests if so young a knight comes to the jousts without a sword. But where can I find him one?... I know! I saw one sticking in an anvil in the churchyard. I'll fetch that: it's doing no good there!"

So Arthur set spurs to his horse and came to the churchyard. Tying his horse to the stile, he ran to the tent which had been set over the stone—and found that all ten of the guardian knights had also gone to the tournament. Without stopping to read what was written on the stone, Arthur pulled out the sword at a touch, ran back to his horse, and in a few minutes had caught up with Sir Kay and handed it over to him.

Arthur knew nothing of what the sword was, but Kay had already tried to pull it from the anvil, and saw at a glance that it was the same one. Instantly he rode to his father Sir Ector, and said:

"Sir! Look, here is the sword out of the stone! So you see I must be the true-born King of all Britain!"

But Sir Ector knew better than to believe Sir Kay too readily. Instead, he rode back with him to the church, and there made him swear a solemn oath with his hands on the Bible to say truly how he came by the sword.

"My brother Arthur brought it to me," said Kay, with a sigh.

"And how did *you* get the sword?" asked Sir Ector.

"Sir, I will tell you," said Arthur, fearing that he had done wrong.

"Kay sent me to fetch his sword, but I could not come to it. Then I remembered having seen this sword sticking uselessly into an anvil in the churchyard. I thought it could be put to a better use in my brother's hand—so I fetched it."

"Did you find no knights guarding the sword?" asked Sir Ector.

"Never a one," said Arthur.

"Well, put the sword back into the anvil, and let us see you draw it out," commanded Sir Ector.

"That's easily done," said Arthur, puzzled by all this trouble over a sword, and he set it back easily into the anvil.

Then Sir Kay seized it by the hilt and pulled his hardest: but struggle and strain as he might, he could not move it by a hair's breadth. Sir Ector tried also, but with no better success.

"Pull it out," he said to Arthur.

And Arthur, more and more bewildered, put his hand to the hilt and drew forth the sword as if out of a well-greased scabbard.

"Now," said Sir Ector, kneeling before Arthur and bowing his head in reverence, "I understand that you and none other are the true-born King of this land."

"Why? Oh, why is it I? Why do you kneel to me, my father?" cried Arthur.

"It is God's will that whoso might draw forth the sword out of the stone and out of the anvil is the true-born King of Britain," said Sir Ector. "Moreover, though I love you well, you are no son of mine. For Merlin brought you to me when you were a small child, and bade me bring you up as my own son!"

"Then if I am indeed King," said Arthur, bowing his head over the cross-hilt of the sword, "I hereby pledge myself to the service of God and of my people, to the righting of wrongs, to the driving-out of evil, to the bringing of peace and plenty to my land... Good sir, you have been as a father to me since ever I can remember, be still near me with a father's love and a father's counsel and advice... Kay, my foster-brother, be you seneschal over all my lands and a true knight of my court."

After this they went to the Archbishop and told him all. But the knights and barons were filled with rage and jealousy, and refused to believe that Arthur was the true-born King. So the choice was put off until Easter; and at Easter once more until Whitsun, or Pentecost as it then was called: but still, though many kings and knights came to try their strength, Arthur alone could pull out the sword.

Then all the people cried: "Arthur! We will have Arthur! By God's will he is our King! God save King Arthur!" And knelt down before him, the noble and the humble together, the rich and the poor, and cried him mercy for delaying him so long. And Arthur forgave them readily, and kneeling down himself he gave the wondrous sword to the Archbishop and received of him the high and holy order of Knighthood. And then came all the earls and the barons, the knights and squires, and did homage to Arthur, swearing to serve and obey him as was their duty.

Merlin told the nobles that Arthur had come to reign over a kingdom greater than all that had gone before; it would be called Logres and it would be a land of blessing, for a little while, before darkness came again. Not all accepted Arthur's rule, yet in time he was victorious against all rebels. Now peace and safety were established, and the court was dedicated to honor and adventure.

At this time, near the beginning of his reign, word came one day to Arthur's castle at Caerleon that a wondrous strong knight, King Pellinore, had set himself up by the high road and sworn to fight all who came against him. Arthur's squire, young Gryflet, begged that he might be knighted at once so that he could fight King Pellinore, and with heavy heart Arthur agreed. Yet for all Sir Gryflet's courage, it took the battle-hardened Pellinore little effort to defeat and wound him grievously.

Arthur was very wroth when he saw how badly hurt was Sir Gryflet, and at once he put on his own armor, closed the vizor of his helmet so that no one could see his face, and with spear in hand rode hard into the forest to be revenged upon King Pellinore.

But on his way he found three robbers attacking Merlin, and they seemed like to beat him to death with great clubs.

"Fly, churls!" cried Arthur, riding at them furiously, and the three cowards turned and fled when they saw the knight charging at them.

"Ah, Merlin," said Arthur, "for all your wisdom and your magic, you would have been murdered in a few minutes if I had not come to your rescue!"

"Not so," answered Merlin, smiling his mysterious smile. "Easily could I have saved myself, had I willed it. It is you who draw near to your death—for you go toward it in your pride, if God does not aid you."

But Arthur would not take heed of Merlin's wisdom, and rode fiercely on until he came to the rich pavilion by the well. And there sat King Pellinore upon his great warhorse, waiting for him.

"Sir knight!" cried Arthur, "why stand you here, fighting and striking down all the knights who ride this way?"

"It is my custom to do so," answered Pellinore sternly. "And if any man would make me change my custom, let him try at his peril!"

"I will make you change it!" cried Arthur.

"And I will defend my custom," replied Pellinore quietly.

Then they drew apart, and came riding together at full tilt, so hard that both spears shivered into little pieces as each hit the center of the other's shield. Arthur would have drawn his sword then, but Pellinore said:

"Not so, let us run together with spears yet again."

"So I would," said Arthur, "If I had another spear!"

"I have plenty," answered Pellinore, and he shouted to his squire to bring two out of the pavilion.

Once more the two kings jousted together; and once more their spears broke into fragments without either of them being struck from his horse. A third time they jousted, and Arthur's spear broke, but King Pellinore's struck him so hard in the middle of the shield that horse and man fell to the earth.

But Arthur sprang to his feet in a great fury, drawing his sword and shouting defiance at Pellinore, who thereupon came down from his horse and drew his own sword. Then began a fierce battle, with many great strokes; they hacked and hewed at one another, cutting pieces off their shields and armor, and suffering each of them so many wounds that the trampled grass in front of the pavilion was stained with red. They rested once, and then charged at each other again: but their swords met together with so mighty a crash that Arthur's broke in two, leaving him with the useless hilt in his hand.

"Ah ha!" cried King Pellinore. "Now you are in my power, to slay or spare as I will! And I will kill you forthwith, unless you kneel and yield to me, confessing yourself to be a knight of little worth."

"There are two ways with that," cried Arthur, mad with shame and fury. "Death is welcome when it comes; but to yield—never!" And with that he leapt in under Pellinore's sword, seized him round the waist and hurled him to the ground. They struggled there for a little while, but Pellinore was still the strongest, and presently he tore off Arthur's helmet and took up his sword to cut his head off also.

But Merlin came suddenly and laid his hand on Pellinore's shoulder: "Knight," he said, "hold your hand and do not strike this stroke. For if you do the hope of Logres dies, and you put this land of Britain into the greatest ruin and desolation that ever a country suffered."

"Who is it?" asked Pellinore.

"This is King Arthur!" said Merlin.

For a moment Pellinore was tempted to strike the blow: for he feared that if Arthur lived, he would never forgive him for what he had done. But Merlin smiled quietly, and placed his hand on Pellinore's head. And at once all the anger and fear went from his mind, and he sank back quietly against the tree beside the well of clear water, and passed into a deep sleep.

Merlin helped King Arthur, who was sorely wounded, to mount his horse, and led him away into the forest.

"Alas, Merlin, what have you done?" asked Arthur; for now he had put from him all the pride and wilfulness which had so nearly caused his death. "You have killed this good knight by your magic—and I would rather have lost my kingdom than that one so brave and mighty should die thus."

"Cease to trouble," said Merlin. "For all things work by the will of God and to the glory of Logres. He is more like to live than you are, for you are sorely wounded, and he does but sleep. . . . I told you how mighty a fighter he was. This is King Pellinore who in time to come shall do you good service. And his sons, Sir Tor and Sir Lamorak, shall be among the bravest of your knights."

Then Merlin brought Arthur to a hermitage where lived a good old man who was a clever leech, or healer of wounds. And in three days he was nearly cured, and could ride once more and fight as strongly as ever.

"Alas," said Arthur as they rode through the forest. "Now I have no sword."

"Let not that trouble you," said Merlin. "There was no virtue in the sword which is lost: it has served its purpose. But near here your own sword awaits you: it was made in Avalon by fairy craft, made for you alone until you must return it ere you journey to Avalon yourself. It is called

Excalibur, and none may stand against its stroke: and with it you shall bring freedom and peace to Logres. This is the hour appointed when Excalibur shall be placed in your hand—for now you will grasp its hilt in all humility, and draw it only to defend the right."

Deeper and deeper into the forest they went, and before long the hills rose on either side until they were riding through a narrow valley that wound through dark mountains. And at last they came to a narrow pass in the rocks, and beyond it, in a cup of mountains, Arthur saw a strange lake. All around it the hills rose darkly and desolately, but the lake water was of the clearest, sunniest blue, and the shore was covered thickly in fresh green grass and flowers. Over the brow of a little rise beyond the lake, the mountains opened out into a great plain, and beyond it was water, half hidden in mist, and broken with many islands.

"This is the Lake of the Fairy Palace," said Merlin, "and beyond the lake, over the brow of the hill yonder, lies the plain of Camlann where the last battle shall be fought, and you shall fall beneath the stroke of the Evil Knight. And beyond the plain lies Avalon, hidden in the mist and the mysterious waters. . . . Go down now and speak with the Lady of the Lake, while I wait for you here."

Leaving his horse with Merlin, Arthur went down the steep path to the side of the magic lake. Standing on the shore, he looked out across the quiet blue water—and there in the very center of the Lake he saw an arm clothed in white samite with a hand holding above the surface a wondrous sword with a golden hilt set with jewels, and a jeweled scabbard and belt.

And then Arthur saw a beautiful damsel dressed in pale blue silk with a golden girdle, who walked across the water until she stood before him on the shore.

"I am the Lady of the Lake," she said, "and I am come to tell you that your sword Excalibur awaits you yonder. Do you wish to take the sword and wear it at your side?"

"Damsel," said Arthur, "that is indeed my wish."

"For long I have guarded the sword," said the Lady of the Lake. "Give me but a gift when I shall come to ask you for one, and the sword shall be yours."

"By my faith," answered Arthur, "I swear to give you whatsoever gift you shall ask for."

"Enter into this boat, then," said the Lady of the Lake. And Arthur saw a barge floating on the water before him, into which he stepped. The Lady of the Lake stood on the shore behind him, but the barge moved across the water as if unseen hands drew it by the keel, until Arthur came beside the arm clothed in white samite. Leaning out, he took the sword and the scabbard: and at once the arm and the hand which had held it sank quietly out of sight beneath the blue waters.

Then the barge brought Arthur to the shore where the Lady of the Lake had stood: but now she was gone also. He tied the barge to a tree root which curved over the waterside, and strode joyfully up the steep path to the pass, buckling the sword Excalibur to his side as he went.

Merlin awaited him with the horses, and together they rode away into the forest, and back by many winding paths until they drew near the river which lay between them and Caerleon, and came to the straight, paved road leading to the city.

"In a little while," said Merlin, "King Pellinore will come riding toward us. For he has ceased to do battle with all who pass through the forest, having seen a Questing Beast which he must follow now for many years."

"Then I will fight with him once more," cried Arthur. "Now that I have so good a sword as Excalibur, maybe I shall overcome and slay him!"

Merlin shook his head: "Let him pass," he said, "for so I counsel you. He is a brave knight and a mighty, and in days to come he will do you good service, and he and his sons shall be among the bravest in your court."

"I will do as you advise me," said Arthur. But he looked upon the sword Excalibur, and sighed.

"Which like you better, the sword or the scabbard?" asked Merlin.

"I like the sword!" cried Arthur.

"Then are you the more unwise," said Merlin gravely. "The scabbard is worth ten such swords: for while you wear that magic scabbard you shall lose but little blood, however sorely you are wounded. Keep well that scabbard, and have good care of it after I am gone from you, for a certain wicked lady who is nearly related to you shall seek to steal both sword and scabbard."

They rode on, and in a little while met King Pellinore—who rode past as if he had not see them.

"I marvel," said Arthur, "that he did not even speak to us!"

"He saw you not," answered Merlin, "for my magic was upon him. But had you striven to stay him in your pride, then he would have seen you well enough."

Before long they came to Caerleon, and his knights welcomed Arthur joyfully. And when they heard of his adventures, they were surprised that he should thus have gone into danger alone. But all the bravest and noblest of them rejoiced exceedingly that they had such a king, one who would risk his life in an adventure as other ordinary knights did.

Guinevere

The tragic story of Guinevere, Arthur's queen, has fascinated people for centuries. She loved Sir Launcelot, the greatest of all Arthur's knights. It was Arthur's tragedy that his personal life was unhappy: next to Guinevere, he loved Launcelot best of all people in the world.

Both Guinevere and Launcelot honored the king, but their love for each other was beyond their power to control. King Arthur avoided facing what he knew, because he did not want to force a confrontation that could only bring tragedy. Tragedy came nonetheless, and the love between Guinevere and Launcelot was the occasion of the civil war that destroyed the brotherhood of the Round Table.

ADVENTURES AND
WONDER TALES

Myths do many things. They explain how things came to be the way they are, tell of the struggle between good and evil forces in the world, and give us gods and heroes in all their glory and inconsistency. But one of the reasons myths are remembered and enjoyed is because they are good stories.

The adventurers you'll meet in this chapter are both human beings and gods. They are in search of something, or seek adventure, or perhaps they just want to reach home safely. All experience wonders and must meet challenges they never imagined. At the end, they all return home, having learned something about themselves and about existence from their experiences.

The Orphan Boy and the Elk Dogs

BY RICHARD ERDOES
AND ALFONSO ORTIZ

In this story, the despised outcast brings the people one of their greatest gifts.

In the days when people had only dogs to carry their bundles, two orphan children, a boy and his sister, were having a hard time. The boy was deaf, and because he could not understand what people said, they thought him foolish and dull-witted. Even his relatives wanted nothing to do with him. The name he had been given at birth, while his parents still lived, was Long Arrow. Now he was like a beaten, mangy dog, the kind who hungrily roams outside a camp, circling it from afar, smelling the good meat boiling in the kettles but never coming close for fear of being kicked. Only his sister, who was bright and beautiful, loved him.

Then the sister was adopted by a family from another camp, people who were attracted by her good looks and pleasing ways. Though they wanted her for a daughter, they certainly did not want the awkward, stupid boy. And so they took away the only person who cared about him, and the orphan boy was left to fend for himself. He lived on scraps thrown to the dogs and things he found on the refuse heaps. He dressed in remnants of skins and frayed robes discarded by the poorest people. At night he bedded down in a grass-lined dugout, like an animal in its den.

Eventually the game was hunted out near the camp that the boy regarded as his, and the people decided to move. The lodges were taken down, belongings were packed into rawhide bags and put on dog travois, and the village departed. "Stay here," they told the boy. "We don't want your kind coming with us."

For two or three days the boy fed on scraps the people had left behind, but he knew he would starve if he stayed. He had to join his people, whether they liked it or not. He followed their tracks, frantic that he would lose them, and crying at the same time. Soon the sweat was running down his skinny body. As he was stumbling, running, panting, something suddenly snapped in his left ear with a sound like a small crack, and a wormlike substance came out of that ear. All at once on his left side he could hear birdsongs for the first time. He took this wormlike thing in his left hand and hurried on. Then there was a snap in his right ear and a wormlike thing came out of it, and on his right side he could hear the rushing waters of a stream. His hearing was restored! And it was razor-sharp—he could make out the rustling of a tiny mouse in dry leaves a good distance away. The orphan boy laughed and was happy for the first time in his life. With renewed courage he followed the trail his people had made.

In the meantime the village had settled into its new place. Men were already out hunting. Thus the boy came upon Good Running, a kindly old chief, butchering a fat buffalo cow he had just killed. When the chief saw the boy, he said to himself, "Here comes that poor good-for-nothing boy. It was wrong to abandon him." To the boy Good Running said, "Rest here, grandson, you're sweaty and covered with dust. Here, have some tripe."

The boy wolfed down the meat. He was not used to hearing and talking yet, but his eyes were alert, and Good Running also noticed a change in his manner. "This boy," the chief said to himself, "is neither stupid nor crazy." He gave the orphan a piece of the hump meat, then a piece of liver, then a piece of raw kidney, and at last the very best kind of meat—a slice of tongue. The more the old man looked at the boy, the more he liked him. On the spur of the moment he said, "Grandson, I'm going to adopt you; there's a place for you in my teepee. And I'm going to make you into a good hunter and warrior." The boy wept, this time for joy. Good Running said, " They called you a stupid, crazy boy, but now that I think of it, the name you were given at birth is Long Arrow. I'll see that people call you by your right name. Now come along."

So a new life began for Long Arrow. He had to learn to speak and to understand well, and to catch up on all the things a boy should know. He was a fast learner and soon surpassed other boys his age in knowledge and skills. At last even Good Running's wife accepted him.

He grew up into a fine young hunter, tall and good-looking in the quilled buckskin outfit the chief's wife made for him. He helped his grandfather in everything and became a staff for Good Running to lean on. But he was lonely, for most people in the camp could not forget that Long Arrow had once been an outcast. "Grandfather," he said one day, "I want to do something to make you proud and show people that you were wise to adopt me. What can I do?"

Good Running answered, "Someday you will be a chief and do great things."

"But what's a great thing I could do now, Grandfather?"

The chief thought for a long time. "Maybe I shouldn't tell you this," he said. "I love you and don't want to lose you. But on winter nights, men talk of powerful spirit people living at the bottom of a faraway lake. Down in that lake the spirit people keep mystery animals who do their work for them. These animals are larger than a great elk, but they carry the burdens of the spirit people like dogs. So they're called Pono-Kamita—Elk Dogs. They are said to be swift, strong, gentle, and beautiful beyond imagination. Every fourth generation, one of our young warriors has gone to find these spirit folk and bring back an Elk Dog for us. But none of our brave young men has ever returned."

"Grandfather, I'm not afraid. I'll go and find the Elk Dog."

"Grandson, first learn to be a man. Learn the right prayers and ceremonies. Be brave. Be generous and open-handed. Pity the old and the fatherless, and let the holy men of the tribe find a medicine for you which will protect you on your dangerous journey. We will begin by purifying you in the sweat bath."

So Long Arrow was purified with the white steam of the sweat lodge. He was taught how to use the pipe, and how to pray to the Great Mystery Power. The tribe's holy men gave him a medicine and made for him a shield with designs on it to ward off danger.

Then one morning, without telling anybody, Good Running loaded his best travois dog with all the things Long Arrow would need for traveling. The chief gave him his medicine, his shield, and his own fine bow and, just as the sun came up, went with his grandson to the edge of the camp to purify him with sweet-smelling cedar smoke. Long Arrow left unheard and unseen by anyone else. After a while some people noticed that he was gone, but no one except his grandfather knew where and for what purpose.

Following Good Running's advice, Long Arrow wandered southward. On the fourth day of his journey he came to a small pond, where a strange man was standing as if waiting for him. "Why have you come here?" the stranger asked.

"I have come to find the mysterious Elk Dog."

"Ah, there I cannot help you," said the man, who was the spirit of the pond. "But if you travel further south, four-times-four days, you might chance upon a bigger lake and there meet one of my uncles. Possibly he might talk to you; then again, he might not. That's all I can tell you."

Long Arrow wandered on, walking for long hours and taking little time for rest. Through deep canyons and over high mountains he went, wearing out his moccasins and enduring cold and heat, hunger and thirst.

Finally Long Arrow approached a big lake surrounded by steep pine-covered hills. There he came face to face with a tall man, fierce and scowling, and twice the height of most humans. This stranger carried a long lance with a heavy spearpoint made of shining flint. "Young one," he growled, "why did you come here?"

"I came to find the mysterious Elk Dog."

The stranger, who was the spirit of the lake, stuck his face right into Long Arrow's and shook his mighty lance. "Little one, aren't you afraid of me?" he snarled.

"No, I am not," answered Long Arrow, smiling.

The tall spirit man gave a hideous grin, which was his way of being friendly. "I like small humans who aren't afraid," he said, "but I can't help you. Perhaps our grandfather will take the trouble to listen to you. More likely he won't. Walk south for four-times-four days, and maybe you'll find him. But probably you won't." With that the tall spirit turned his back on Long Arrow and went to the bottom of the lake, where he lived.

Long Arrow walked on for another four-times-four days, sleeping and resting little. By now he staggered and stumbled in his weakness, and his dog was not much better off. At last he came to the biggest lake he had ever seen, surrounded by towering snow-capped peaks and waterfalls of ice. This time there was nobody to receive him. As a matter of fact, there seemed to be no living thing around. "This must be the Great Mystery

Lake," thought Long Arrow. Exhausted, he fell down upon the shortgrass meadow by the lake, fell down among the wild flowers, and went to sleep with his tired dog curled up at his feet.

When Long Arrow awoke, the sun was already high. He opened his eyes and saw a beautiful child standing before him, a boy in a dazzling white buckskin robe decorated with porcupine quills of many colors. The boy said, "We have been expecting you for a long time. My grandfather invites you to his lodge. Follow me."

Telling his dog to wait, Long Arrow took his medicine shield and his grandfather's bow and went with the wonderful child. They came to the edge of the lake. The spirit boy pointed to the water and said, "My grandfather's lodge is down there. Come!" The child turned himself into a kingfisher and dove straight to the bottom.

Afraid, Long Arrow thought, "How can I follow him and not be drowned?" But then he said to himself, "I knew all the time that this would not be easy. In setting out to find the Elk Dog, I already threw my life away." And he boldly jumped into the water. To his surprise, he found it did not make him wet, that it parted before him, that he could breathe and see. He touched the lake's sandy bottom. It sloped down, down toward a center point.

Long Arrow descended this slope until he came to a small flat valley. In the middle of it stood a large teepee of tanned buffalo hide. The images of two strange animals were drawn on it in sacred vermilion paint. A kingfisher perched high on the top of the teepee flew down and turned again into the beautiful boy, who said, "Welcome. Enter my grandfather's lodge."

Long Arrow followed the spirit boy inside. In the back at the seat of honor sat a black-robed old man with flowing white hair and such power emanating from him that Long Arrow felt himself in the presence of a truly Great One. The holy man welcomed Long Arrow and offered him food. The man's wife came in bringing dishes of buffalo hump, liver, tongues, delicious chunks of deer meat, the roasted flesh of strange, tasty water birds, and meat pounded together with berries, chokecherries, and kidney fat. Famished after his long journey, Long Arrow ate with relish. Yet he still looked around to admire the furnishings of the teepee, the painted inner curtain, the many medicine shields, wonderfully wrought weapons, shirts and robes decorated with porcupine quills in rainbow colors, beautifully painted rawhide containers filled with wonderful things, and much else that dazzled him.

After Long Arrow had stilled his hunger, the old spirit chief filled the pipe and passed it to his guest. They smoked, praying silently. After a while the old man said, "Some came before you from time to time, but they were always afraid of the deep water, and so they went away with empty hands. But you, grandson, were brave enough to plunge in, and therefore you are chosen to receive a wonderful gift to carry back to your people. Now, go outside with my grandson."

The beautiful boy took Long Arrow to a meadow on which some strange animals, unlike any the young man had ever seen, were galloping and gamboling, neighing and nickering. They were truly wonderful to look at, with their glossy coats fine as a maiden's hair, their long manes and tails streaming in the wind. Now rearing, now nuzzling, they looked at Long Arrow with gentle eyes which belied their fiery appearance.

"At last," thought Long Arrow, "here they are before my own eyes, the Pono-Kamita, the Elk Dogs!"

"Watch me," said the mystery boy, "so that you learn to do what I am doing." Gracefully and without effort, the boy swung himself onto the back of a jet-black Elk Dog with a high, arched neck. Larger than any elk Long Arrow had ever come across, the animal carried the boy all over the meadow swiftly as the wind. Then the boy returned, jumped off his mount, and said, "Now you try it." A little timidly Long Arrow climbed up on the beautiful Elk Dog's back. Seemingly regarding him as feather-light, it took off like a flying arrow. The young man felt himself soaring through the air as a bird does, and experienced a happiness greater even than the joy he had felt when Good Running had adopted him as a grandson.

When they had finished riding the Elk Dogs, the spirit boy said to Long Arrow, "Young hunter from the land above the waters, I want you to have what you have come for. Listen to me. You may have noticed that my grandfather wears a black medicine robe as long as a woman's dress, and that he is always trying to hide his feet. Try to get a glimpse of them, for if you do, he can refuse you nothing. He will then tell you to ask him for a gift, and you must ask for these three things: his rainbow-colored quilled belt, his black medicine robe, and a herd of these animals which you seem to like."

Long Arrow thanked him and vowed to follow his advice. For four days the young man stayed in the spirit chief's lodge, where he ate well and often went out riding on the Elk Dogs. But try as he would, he could never get a look at the old man's feet. The spirit chief always kept them carefully covered. Then on the morning of the fourth day, the old one was walking out of the teepee when his medicine robe caught in the entrance flap. As the robe opened, Long Arrow caught a glimpse of a leg and one foot. He was awed to see that it was not a human limb at all, but the glossy leg and firm hoof of an Elk Dog! He could not stifle a cry of surprise, and the old man looked over his shoulder and saw that his leg and hoof were exposed. The chief seemed a little embarrassed, but shrugged and said, "I tried to hide this, but you must have been fated to see it. Look, both of my feet are those of an Elk Dog. You may as well ask me for a gift. Don't be timid; tell me what you want."

Long Arrow spoke boldly: "I want three things: your belt of rainbow colors, your black medicine robe, and your herd of Elk Dogs."

"Well, so you're really not timid at all!" said the old man. "You ask for a lot, and I'll give you half of them. Now I must tell you that my black medicine robe and my many-colored belt have Elk Dog magic in them. Always wear the robe when you try to catch Elk Dogs; then they can't get away from you. On quiet nights, if you listen closely to the belt, you will hear the Elk Dog dance song and Elk Dog prayers. You must learn them. And I will give you one more magic gift: this long rope woven from the hair of a white buffalo bull. With it you will never fail to catch whichever Elk Dog you want."

The spirit chief presented him with the gifts and said, "Now you must leave. At first the Elk Dogs will not follow you. Keep the medicine robe and the magic belt on at all times, and walk for four days toward the north. Never look back—always look to the north. On the fourth day the Elk Dogs will come up beside you on the left. Still don't look back. But after they have overtaken you, catch one with the rope of white buffalo hair and ride him home. Don't lose the black robe, or you will lose the Elk Dogs and never catch them again."

Long Arrow listened carefully so that he would remember. Then the old spirit chief had his wife make up a big pack of food, almost too heavy for Long Arrow to carry, and the young man took leave of his generous spirit host. The mysterious boy once again turned himself into a king-fisher and led Long Arrow to the surface of the lake, where his faithful dog greeted him joyfully. Long Arrow fed the dog, put his pack of food on the travois, and started walking north.

On the fourth day the Elk Dogs came up on his left side, as the spirit chief had foretold. Long Arrow snared the black one with the arched neck to ride, and he caught another to carry the pack of food. They galloped swiftly on, the dog barking at the big Elk Dogs' heels.

When Long Arrow arrived at last in his village, the people were afraid and hid. They did not recognize him astride his beautiful Elk Dog but took him for a monster, half man and half animal. Long Arrow kept calling, "Grandfather Good Running, it's your grandson. I've come back bringing Elk Dogs!"

Recognizing the voice, Good Running came out of hiding and wept for joy, because he had given Long Arrow up for lost. Then all the others emerged from their hiding places to admire the wonderful new animals.

Long Arrow said, "My grandfather and grandmother who adopted me, I can never repay you for your kindness. Accept these wonderful Elk Dogs as my gift. Now we no longer need to be humble foot-sloggers, because these animals will carry us swiftly everywhere we want to go. Now buffalo hunting will be easy. Now our teepees will be larger, our possessions will be greater, because an Elk Dog travois can carry a load ten times bigger than that of a dog. Take them, my grandparents. I shall keep for myself only this black male and this black female, which will grow into a fine herd."

"You have indeed done something great, grandson," said Good Running, and he spoke true. The people became the bold riders of the Plains, and soon could hardly imagine how they had existed without these wonderful animals.

After some time Good Running, rich and honored by all, said to Long Arrow, "Grandson, lead us to the Great Mystery Lake so we can camp by its shores. Let's visit the spirit chief and the wondrous boy; maybe they will give us more of their power and magic gifts." Long Arrow led the people southward and again found the Great Mystery Lake. But the waters would no longer part for him, nor would any of the kingfishers they saw turn into a boy. Nor, gazing down into the crystal-clear water, could they discover people, Elk Dogs, or a teepee. There was nothing in the lake but a few fish.

The Elk Dogs

There were no horses in the Americas until the Spanish brought them to Mexico in 1519, and escaped horses ran wild. The Blackfoot did not encounter horses and domesticate them until around 1725. This myth therefore was created at that time, or shortly after.

It is said that when the Aztecs first saw Spanish soldiers mounted on horseback, they thought they were monsters, half man and half animal. The theme of the outcast orphan boy who becomes a hero is very common in Native North American stories, particularly on the Plains.

Thor's Visit to Utgard

BY ROGER LANCELYN GREEN

Like Odin, Thor liked to travel through the different worlds in search of adventure. One time he set off to visit Utgard, the castle of the giants. Who should go with him but Loki the trickster— not the first time these two traveled in each other's company, and not the last. Æsir (pronounced EE-sir) means "gods"; the singular is Asa.

In the evening they came to a farmhouse on the edge of the river Ifing, the dark flood that never froze, which separated Midgard [earth] from Jotunheim [land of the giants]. The good yeoman to whom it belonged welcomed his two strange guests, but confessed that he had very little food in the house, indeed scarcely enough for himself and his son and daughter, Thialfi and Roskva.

"That is no matter!" cried Thor, and killing his two goats Gaptooth and Cracktooth, he helped to flay and joint them. Very soon they were simmering in the pot, and the dinner was ready.

"Whatever you do," Thor remarked, "let none of the bones of my goats be broken." Then the meal began, and Thor showed his usual good appetite by eating one whole goat and a good deal of the other.

"What he said about the bones is only to keep the marrow for himself," whispered Loki the tempter to Thialfi, "for it has strange and wonderful powers, since these are no ordinary goats."

So Thialfi split one of the thigh bones when Thor was looking the other way, and scraped out some of the marrow with his knife. But he noticed that Loki was careful not to break any of the bones, so he contented himself with the one taste of marrow.

Thor and Loki slept that night in the farmhouse, and in the morning Thor flung all the bones into the goatskins, waved his hammer Miolnir over them, and at once Gaptooth and Cracktooth sprang up as full of life as ever. But one of them limped a little in his hind leg, and seeing this Thor turned with a roar of fury and whirled his hammer above his head to slay the yeoman and his two children.

"One of you has broken the thigh bone!" he shouted, his eyes flashing fire and his knuckles growing white as he gripped Miolnir. The yeoman cowered on the floor, realizing who his terrible guest was, and promised any recompense he chose to ask.

Seeing the man's fear, Thor's brow cleared and he said: "I will not smite. But your two children Thialfi and Roskva shall come with me, he to be my squire and she my handmaiden for evermore. See, it is an honor I do them and no evil. . . . Now look well to my goats so that the bone is set and whole before our return. Roskva shall remain with you until then, but Thialfi comes with us now."

So Thor and Loki continued their journey on foot, with Thialfi to attend on them. They went down beside the river Ifing until they reached the sea, and crossed where it was deepest in a boat that lay waiting for them. On the further shore they left the boat and advanced inland through a great forest. As evening approached they came out into open country among bare rocks and dark valleys, but nowhere could they find a house.

At last, just as darkness was beginning to fall and they were feeling exceedingly tired and hungry, they came to a strange building. It was a great hall with an entrance so wide that it took up the whole end, but there was no one in it, no hearth nor fire, and no furniture. It was better than nothing, however, in that freezing land, and the wayfarers made themselves as comfortable as possible in their strange lodging.

In the middle of the night they were wakened suddenly by a great earthquake, the ground shook all round them, and the hall trembled and swayed from side to side. Nothing else happened, but as he was exploring further Thor found a smaller room leading off the hall on the right-hand side, and into this his companions moved for greater warmth. Loki and the boy huddled together in the furthest corner, shaking with fear, but Thor gripped the handle of Miolnir firmly and stood on guard in the doorway.

He could hear a roaring and a bellowing sound nearby, and from time to time a great crash: but he could see nothing.

At last the sky turned gray, and going out of the hall Thor saw in the first light of morning a Giant lying on the hillside a little distance away, snoring loudly. He was not a small Giant by any means—indeed he was the largest that Thor had ever seen. Then Thor knew what the noises were that he had heard in the night, and in a fit of anger he girded himself with his belt of strength and swung Miolnir in his hands, wondering where to strike.

At that moment the Giant woke, and Thor decided that it was safer not to use his hammer just then. Instead he asked: "Who are you that have disturbed our slumbers with your snores?"

"I am Skrymir," answered the Giant in a voice that echoed among the mountains. "I have come to lead you to Utgard. I need not ask if you are Thor, for your hammer betrays you. But indeed you are rather smaller than I expected.... Hallo, what have you been doing with my glove?"

With that he picked up what Thor had taken for a hall, shook Loki and Thialfi out of it, and put it on, slipping his thumb into the room where they had passed the night.

Then he opened his bag and made a huge breakfast, leaving Thor and his companions to be content with what they could find.

"I'll carry your bag of provisions in my own," said Skrymir, when he had finished his breakfast. "Then we can dine together tonight in a more friendly fashion." Thor agreed readily, and Thialfi handed over the empty wallet, which Skrymir dropped into his own bag before lacing up the top and slinging it over his shoulder.

"Now follow me!" he boomed, and went striding away over the mountains while Thor and Loki did their best to keep up with him, and Thialfi followed painfully behind—though indeed he was the swiftest-footed of all men.

Late in the evening Skrymir found them shelter for the night under a mighty oak tree where they could get out of the bitter wind among its roots, and he lay on the hillside beyond its huge trunk.

"I am too tired to bother about supper," said the Giant as he stretched himself out. "But here is the food-bag: open it and help yourselves." He flung down his sack, and a few moments later was snoring like a volcano on the other side of the tree.

Thor set himself to unlace the food-bag; but pull and lever as he might, not a single thong could he loosen. Nor could he cut through the stiff leather.

"This Giant is mocking us!" he exclaimed at last, and in a rage he rushed round the tree and hit Skrymir on the head with Miolnir.

The Giant stirred in his sleep, yawned, and muttered sleepily: "That was a big leaf which dropped on my head!... What are you doing, Thor? You have finished supper, I suppose, and are ready for bed?"

"We're just thinking about going to sleep," growled Thor, and when Skrymir was snoring once more, he led Loki and Thialfi to another oak tree at a little distance where they settled down in hungry discomfort to get what rest they could.

Midnight came, and Thor still could not sleep. Giant Skrymir had rolled on to his back and was snoring until the trees shook as if a great storm was raging.

"I'll silence that monster!" grumbled Thor. "If we cannot eat, we might at least get a little sleep!"

He strode round to where Skrymir lay, planted his feet firmly, whirled Miolnir round his head and struck him on the crown with all his strength so that the hammerhead sank almost out of sight.

"What's happening now?" asked the Giant, sitting up. "Curse this oak tree! An acorn landed right on my head and woke me!... Or was it you, Thor, with news of some danger threatening us?"

"There's no danger that I know of," answered Thor. "It's now about midnight, and I had just woken and was stretching my legs for a few moments."

Skrymir grunted, and went to sleep again; but Thor, bristling with fury, sat with hammer in hand, planning how he would strike one more blow which should make an end of the Giant. "If I can strike a really good one," he thought to himself, "he shall never see the light of day again!"

When dawn was just beginning to break Thor decided that his time had come. Skrymir appeared to be sleeping soundly, lying in such a way that Thor could reach one of his temples quite easily. So he rushed upon him whirling Miolnir with all his strength, and delivered a crashing blow.

Skrymir sat up suddenly and rubbed his head. "It's those birds up in the oak tree!" he exclaimed. "One of them dropped a twig on my forehead.... Ah, Thor! So you're awake already. A good thing, for we have a long journey before us if you are to reach Utgard before night."

They continued all day across the mountains, but as afternoon was advancing, Skrymir stopped and said to Thor: "I must leave you here and go northwards. If you turn east you will reach Utgard before evening. But before we part, let me give you some advice. I heard you talking among yourselves and remarking that you had seen Giants smaller than I am. Let me warn you that in the castle of Utgard you will find several far taller than I. So when you get there be careful not to utter boastful words—for the followers of Utgardhaloki [the Giant King] will not take them from such mere babes as you.... In fact, my advice would be to turn back while you have the chance, and get home as quickly as you can."

With that, Skrymir slung his bag over his shoulder, and strode away toward the snow-covered mountains of the far north. And neither Thor nor Loki nor Thialfi was sorry to see him go.

They did not turn back, however, but went on toward the east, and as night was falling they came to a castle which was so high that it hurt the backs of their necks to look up to the top of it. There was an iron grating in the gateway, and this was closed. Thor strained his hardest to open it, but in vain: however, they soon found that they were small enough to squeeze between the bars.

Inside they saw a mighty hall with wide-open doors, and on walking into it found many Giants sitting on benches along either side while Utgardhaloki, the Giant King, sat at the high table on the dais at the end.

Thor and Loki saluted him politely, but at first he took no notice of them and went on picking his teeth. At length, however, he smiled at them scornfully, and said: "As you seem to have come on a long journey, I suppose you are the Æsir from Asgard, and this small boy here must be Thor himself. Perhaps, however, you are greater than you seem: so tell us if you pride yourselves on any special accomplishments. We are all skilled here in feats of strength and endurance, and in craft and cunning as well. Now which of you will challenge one of us to prove his worth?"

"That I will!" cried Loki. "There is one craft in which I excel, particularly at the moment, and that is eating. I'll have an eating match with any of you, and wager that no one can eat faster than I."

"Well, that is a good contest," said Utgardhaloki, "and we will put you to the test at once. Our champion eater is called Logi, and he is ready to eat against you or anyone at any time."

Then a great wooden trough was placed in the middle of the floor and filled with meat, and Loki sat down at one end and Logi at the other. Each set to work as fast as he could, and they met exactly in the middle.

"But Logi has won," Utgardhaloki pointed out. "For while Loki ate only the flesh, leaving the bare bones on the dish, Logi ate bones and dish and all!"

Presently Utgardhaloki looked at Thialfi and said: "And this child? Is there anything he can do?"

"I'll run a race with any one of you who cares to try," answered Thialfi boldly.

"A good accomplishment is running," said Utgardhaloki, "but you must be very swift if you are to outdistance my champion."

Then he led the way out of the hall to a long strip of ground inside the castle walls. "We will put you to the test at once," he said, and called for Hugi, a young Giant, and bade him race with Thialfi.

The course was set and the two runners sped away. But in the first heat Hugi was so much ahead that when he reached the winning post he turned round and went back to meet Thialfi.

Then said Utgardhaloki: "You will need to exert yourself a bit more, Thialfi, if you are to beat Hugi—though no one who has come here has ever run faster than you have just done. Now try a second heat."

They set off again, but this time Hugi reached the end of the course so long before Thialfi that he had time to turn and meet him a quarter of the way back.

"Thialfi has run this heat well also," said Utgardhaloki, "but I do not think that he can beat Hugi. However, he may have one more chance, and that shall decide the match."

They set off for the third time, but now Hugi ran so fast that he was able to reach the winning post, turn round, and meet Thialfi halfway back along the course.

"So Hugi is a better runner than Thialfi," said Utgardhaloki, as he led the way back into the hall. "But these were only small contests. Thor, I am certain, will wish to show his strength, for we have heard great tales of his mighty deeds—and indeed we know that he has won victories against a Giant or two before now."

"We came here in peace, and not to perform the deeds of war," said

Thor warily. "But I am quite ready to contend with anyone in a drinking match."

"An excellent notion," cried Utgardhaloki, and he bade one of his servants bring in the sconce-horn which was handed round among his warriors when they boasted of their powers of drinking. "If one of us drinks this horn empty at a single draught," he said, "we think well of him. Many a Giant, however, needs to pull at it twice; but we think very little of anyone who needs to raise it to his lips a third time."

Thor took the horn, and it did not seem particularly big, except for its great length. He was very thirsty, and as he raised it to his lips he was confident that he would need to take no second draught to empty it. But when his breath failed and he raised his head from the horn and looked to see how much he had drunk, it seemed hardly any emptier than when he started.

"That was well drunk," exclaimed Utgardhaloki, "and yet it was not much. I would not have believed if I had not actually seen it that Thor of Asgard was so poor a drinker. Still, I feel sure you are only waiting to drain the horn at your next draught."

Thor answered nothing, but raised the horn to his lips again, thinking that he would drink deeply indeed this time, and he strained at it until his breath gave out. Yet as he took the horn from his lips he realized that the end had not tilted up as far as it should; and when he came to look inside, it seemed as if less had gone than before: but now he could at least see below the rim.

"How now, Thor!" cried Utgardhaloki. "You'll drink again, surely, even if the third draught is more than is good for you? The third will surely be the greatest—but even if you empty the horn this time, you are not so mighty a champion as you are said to be among the Æsir. Though what you may yet do in other contests remains to be seen."

At that Thor became angry. He raised the horn again and drank with all his might, straining until he could hold his breath no longer. He set down the horn and as he drew back gasping, he saw that at least the liquid in it had sunk quite a distance from the top. But he would not try again, and declared that he had drunk enough for one night.

"Now it is evident that you are not as mighty as we thought," remarked Utgardhaloki. "You cannot even swallow a little drink such as

this. But will you try your hand at other games? You may do better in some feat of strength."

"We hardly call such drinks as that little ones in Asgard," grumbled Thor. "But what game do you suggest now to try my strength?"

"Young lads here," said Utgardhaloki, "begin by a small trial of strength, which is to lift my cat off the ground. I would not suggest so easy a test to Thor of the Æsir, did I not realize how very much less powerful you are than I expected."

As he said this an enormous gray cat leapt into the middle of the floor and stood there spitting. Thor went forward and set his hands under its belly meaning to lift it by the middle. But the cat arched its back as Thor lifted, and though he strained upwards with all his strength he could only raise one paw off the ground.

"It is just as I expected," smiled Utgardhaloki. "But indeed my cat is a very large one, and our people are big and strong, not weak and puny like Thor the Thunderer."

"Small as I am," shouted Thor, "I'll wrestle with any of you. For now you have angered me, and my strength grows double!"

"I see no Giant here who would not think it a disgrace to wrestle with such a midget," said Utgardhaloki, looking round the hall. "But we must not be deceived by appearances. Summon my old nurse, Elli, and let Thor wrestle with her. She has thrown men who seemed to me no less mighty than this great god of Asgard."

Straightway there came into the hall an old woman, bent and stricken with years. Thor flushed angrily when he saw her, but Utgard-haloki insisted on the match, and when at last Thor took hold of her and tried to throw her, he discovered that it was not as easily done as he expected. In fact, the harder he gripped her the firmer she stood; and when she caught hold of him in her turn, Thor felt himself tottering on his feet, and in spite of all he could do she brought him to his knees.

"Enough of this!" cried Utgardhaloki. "It is useless for Thor to try his strength with any of my warriors since he cannot even hold his own against this old woman. Sit down now, all three of you, and let us eat and drink. Only Loki has eaten and only Thor has drunk; but doubtless you can both take more of food and ale—for I would like you to see how well we in Utgard can entertain our guests."

So they made good cheer far into the night, and slept there in the hall. And in the morning, when they were dressed and ready, Utgardhaloki drank a parting cup with them, and led them out of Utgard and well on their way back toward Midgard.

When he turned to bid them farewell, he said: "Now tell me, before we part, what you think of my castle of Utgard and the greatest of the Giant kind who live there? Do you admit that you have at last met Giants who are mightier than you?"

"I must confess," said Thor sadly, "that I have got little but shame from my dealings with you. When I am gone you will speak of me as a weakling, and I am ill content with that. It was with a very different purpose that I came to visit Utgard as the envoy of the Æsir."

"Now I will tell you the truth," said Utgardhaloki, "since you are well away from my castle—which, if it is in my power, you shall never enter again. Indeed had I known how mighty you were, you had never come here at all: for so great is your strength that you have put us and all the world in deadly peril.

"Know then that I have cheated you with false seemings and illusions of the eye. To go back to the beginning: it was I who met you on the way, calling myself Skrymir; and as for my provision-bag, it was tied with iron made by Trolls—so that you could not possibly have untied it. Of the three blows you dealt me with your hammer Miolnir, the first was far the lightest, but it would have killed me if it had really landed on me. On your way home you will see a long mountain shaped like a saddle, with three deep gorges in it, one far deeper than the rest: those gorges you made with your hammer, for in each case I slipped aside so that the mountain received the blows and not I.

"In the same way I cheated you over your contests in my castle hall. The Giant against whom Loki ate so well was called Logi—and he was Fire itself which burned up the trough and bones as well as the meat. Thialfi ran against Hugi, who is Thought: and no man can run as swiftly as thought.

"When you drank from my horn, and the drink seemed to sink but slowly, you performed a wonder which I should not have believed possible. For the other end of the horn was joined to the sea, and it sank visibly throughout all the world when you drank. You caused the first ebb-tide: and the tides shall ebb and flow for ever more in memory of your deed.

"When you strove to lift my cat we were all in deadly terror. For he was the Midgard Serpent which stretches round the whole world—and when you raised it, the head and tail of Jormungand [the Midgard Serpent] scarcely touched the ground.

"Finally, your last feat was a remarkable as the rest. For Elli with whom you wrestled was Old Age—and yet, she only brought you to your knees, though never a man lived nor shall ever live, who will not at the last be vanquished by Old Age.

"Now we must part, and it will be best for both of us if you never come here to seek me again. Should you do so, I will defend my castle by wiles such as I have already used against you—or by others. But if you stay away from Jotunheim, there may be peace between the Æsir and the Giants."

Then a sudden gust of fury filled Thor, and he whirled up Miolnir to fling at Utgardhaloki, deeming that this time there should be no mistake.

But Utgardhaloki was gone; and suddenly the mist came down from the mountains so that when Thor turned back to destroy the castle of Utgard and crush it to pieces, there was no castle to be seen.

So Thor, Loki, and Thialfi turned and groped their way through the fog, back into the mountains, and they could scarcely see in front of them until they came to the great mountain with the three gorges which Thor had cleft with his hammer.

Beyond it the fog cleared, and they made their way easily enough until they came to the farmhouse where Thor had left his chariot.

How Four Visited Glooscap

COLLECTED BY ELLA
ELIZABETH CLARK

The Micmac creator-hero Glooscap is something like Good Brother in the first myth in this book, "The Woman Who Fell from the Sky." After Glooscap had done his great deeds he left the world behind.

Soon after Glooscap had left the Indians, four men agreed to go in search of him. They did not know where he was, but they knew that he could always be found by those who diligently sought him. For many suns and many moons they journeyed. They started in the spring of one year and kept on searching until midsummer of the next year.

Then the men found a small path in the forest that was marked by blazed trees. Following it they came to a beautiful river, then to a broad and beautiful lake, and soon they reached a long spit of land that ran far out into the water. There they climbed a hill and, looking down from the top of it, they saw smoke rising through the trees. In a short time the men came to a large and well-built wigwam.

Entering it, they found two people. On the right sat a middle-aged man, and on the left a very aged woman, doubled over as if she might be more than one hundred years old. Opposite the door a mat was spread out, as if a third person had a seat there.

The man in the wigwam pleasantly welcomed the four visitors and asked them to be seated. But he did not ask the usual questions as to where they were going or where they had come from. After a while, all heard the sound of an approaching canoe and then footsteps. Soon a young man entered the wigwam, well dressed and manly in form and features. His weapons indicated that he had been hunting, and he told the woman that he had brought home some game.

The old woman, weak and tottering, rose with great difficulty, brought in four or five beavers, and started to prepare them for cooking. But so feeble was she that the young man took the knife from her hands and prepared them himself. In a short time, he set before the hungry guests a large portion of the cooked meat.

For seven days the men were hospitably entertained while they rested from their long journey. The hosts seemed to pay no attention to their worn garments, so full of holes that their skin peeped out in all directions.

One morning the middle-aged man asked the young man to wash their mother's face. As soon as he had done so, her wrinkles vanished and she became young-looking and handsome. Her white hair became black and glossy, and she was dressed in a beautiful robe. Instead of looking old, stooped, and feeble, she now appeared young, straight, and active.

The four visitors looked on in amazement. They knew now that whoever their young host was, he had supernatural powers. Gladly they accepted this invitation to look at the country around his wigwam. Beauty was everywhere. Tall trees with rich foliage and fragrant blossoms stood in rows so straight and far apart that the men could see a long distance in every direction. The air was sweet and balmy. Everything suggested health, repose, and happiness.

After they had enjoyed the scene for a time, their host and guide asked, "Where have you men come from and why are you here?"

"We are in search of Glooscap."

"I am Glooscap," he replied. "What can I do for you?"

"I am a wicked man," said one, "and I have an ugly temper. I wish to be calm, meek, and holy."

"Very well," replied Glooscap. "Your wish shall be granted."

"I am poor," said the second man, "and I find it difficult to make a living. I wish to be rich."

"Very well," replied Glooscap. "Your wish shall be granted."

"I am despised by my people," said the third man. "I wish to be loved and respected."

"Your wish shall be granted."

"I wish to live a long time," said the fourth man.

"You have asked a hard thing," said Glooscap, "but I will see what I can do for you."

Next day the three in the wigwam prepared much food, and all four men feasted before starting forth on their return journey. Then Glooscap led them up a hill, very high and difficult to climb. The ground there was rocky, broken, and unfit for cultivation. On the top of the hill, where the sun would shine from morning until night, Glooscap had the men stop. He went to the one who had asked to live a long time, clasped him around the waist, lifted him from the ground, and then set him down again. Glooscap gave him a twist or two as he moved his own hands upward, and then he moved his clasped hands over the man's head. Thus the visitor was transformed into an old, gnarled cedar tree with limbs growing out, rough and ugly, all the way to the bottom.

"There!" exclaimed Glooscap. "I do not know exactly how many years you will live, but I think you will not be disturbed for a long, long time. No one will have any use for you, and the land around you is of no value. I think you will live to be very, very old."

The three companions were horrified. They not only mourned the loss of their comrade, but they wondered how Glooscap would grant their requests. But he soon calmed their fears. Guiding them back to his lodge, he took three small boxes from his medicine bag and gave one to each of the men. Then he told them to take off their old clothes and put on the new ones which he had ready for them. Each garment was beautifully finished and decorated.

Though now eager to return home, the three men dreaded the long journey that had taken them one whole summer, a winter, and half of a second summer. But Glooscap offered to be their guide. Early next morning, he put on his belt and started off, the three men following. About the middle of the morning they reached the top of a high mountain, from which they could see another high mountain in the blue distance.

"It will take us seven suns to reach that mountain," the men said to each other.

Glooscap made no reply, but pushed on. To the astonishment of the three men, they reached the second mountain in the middle of the afternoon.

"Now look round you," directed Glooscap.

"Why, it is our own country!" they exclaimed in surprise.

All below them was familiar. They saw their own hills and forest, their own lake and river. "There is your village," said Glooscap. And then he left them. Before sunset the three men were at home.

At first no one recognized them because of their new and splendid robes. When they explained who they were, they were surrounded by all the people of the village. Men, women, and children listened in amazement to their adventures.

When they finished their story, the men opened their boxes, which Glooscap had said were not to be opened until the travelers reached home. In each was a powerful ointment, which they immediately rubbed over their bodies.

Immediately their wishes were granted. The man who had been hated by his people was made beautiful in spirit and so fragrant from the perfume of the ointment that his company was sought by all and he became greatly loved. The man who had been very poor became a successful hunter and kept his family supplied with an abundance of game. The one who had confessed to a wicked temper became a righteous man, always calm and meek and devout.

They had found Glooscap, and he had granted them their wishes.

The sailors pass by the monster Scylla.

The Voyage of Odysseus

BY PADRAIC COLUM

The wanderings of Odysseus (whom the Romans called Ulysses) are written in Homer's Odyssey, one of humanity's most powerful adventure stories. Many of his trials have become proverbial.

I. The Cyclops

None of the Greek lords in the great war was more dangerous to the Trojans than Odysseus, prince of the small rocky island of Ithaca in western Greece. It was he who devised the plan to build the Trojan Horse. In the storms that scattered the returning Greeks, Odysseus and his men were driven far away from the rest, so far they vanished from the minds of men and seemed lost forever. After years of wandering beyond the limits of the known world, suffering many terrible dangers and the loss of all his comrades, Odysseus was at last washed up on the beaches of the island of Phaeacia, naked and utterly without possessions. The people there received him as an honored guest, and to them, seated in their great hall at night beside their king and queen, he told the story of his wanderings:

"I, whom you see before you as a man destitute of all possessions, dependent on your kindness—I am the many-fabled Odysseus, who was present at the famous sack of Troy. For nine days after we left Troy, almighty Zeus the Cloud-compeller drove us with a terrible north wind, helpless as a swallow that searches wearily among the endless waves for some place to rest its wings...."

"On the tenth day we came to a strange country. Many of my men landed there. The people of that land were harmless and friendly, but the land itself was most dangerous. For there grew there the honey-sweet fruit of the lotus that makes all men forgetful of their past and neglectful of their future. And those of my men who ate the lotus that the dwellers of that land offered them became forgetful of their country and of the way before them. They wanted to abide forever in the land of the lotus. They wept when they thought of all the toils before them and of all they had endured. I led them back to the ships, and I had to place them beneath the benches and leave them in bonds. And I commanded those who had ate of the lotus to go at once aboard the ships. Then, when I had got all my men upon the ships, we made haste to sail away.

Later we came to the land of the Cyclopes, a giant people. There is a waste island outside the harbor of their land, and on it there is a well of bright water that has poplars growing round it. We came to that empty island, and we beached our ships and took down our sails.

As soon as the dawn came we went through the empty island, starting the wild goats that were there in flocks, and shooting them with our arrows. We killed so many wild goats there that we had nine for each ship. Afterwards we looked across to the land of the Cyclopes, and we heard the sound of voices and saw the smoke of fires and heard the bleating of flocks of sheep and goats.

I called my companions together and I said, 'It would be well for some of us to go to that other island. With my own ship and with the company that is on it I shall go there. The rest of you abide here. I will find out what manner of men live there, and whether they will treat us kindly and give us gifts that are due to strangers—gifts of provisions for our voyage.'

We embarked and we came to the land. There was a cave near the sea, and round the cave there were mighty flocks of sheep and goats. I took twelve men with me and I left the rest to guard the ship. We went into the cave and found no man there. There were baskets filled with cheeses, and vessels of whey, and pails and bowls of milk. My men wanted me to take some of the cheeses and drive off some of the lambs and kids and come away. But this I would not do, for I would rather that he who owned the stores would give us of his own free will the offerings that are due to strangers.

While we were in the cave, he whose dwelling it was, returned to it. He carried on his shoulder a great pile of wood for his fire. Never in our lives did we see a creature so frightful as this Cyclops was. He was a giant in size, and, what made him terrible to behold, he had but one eye, and that single eye was in his forehead. He cast down on the ground the pile of wood that he carried, making such a din that we fled in terror into the corners and recesses of the cave. Next he drove his flocks into the cave and began to milk his ewes and goats. And when he had the flocks within, he took up a stone that not all our strengths could move and set it as a door to the mouth of the cave.

The Cyclops kindled his fire, and when it blazed up he saw us in the corners and recesses. He spoke to us. We knew not what he said, but our hearts were shaken with terror at the sound of his deep voice.

I spoke to him saying that we were Agamemnon's men on our way home from the taking of Priam's City, and I begged him to deal with us kindly, for the sake of Zeus who is ever in the company of strangers and suppliants. But he answered me saying, 'We Cyclopes pay no heed to Zeus, nor to any of thy gods. In our strength and our power we deem that we are mightier than they. I will not spare thee, neither will I give thee aught for the sake of Zeus, but only as my own spirit bids me. And first I would have thee tell me how you came to our land.'

I knew it would be better not to let the Cyclops know that my ship and my companions were at the harbor of the island. Therefore I spoke to him guilefully, telling him that my ship had been broken on the rocks, and that I and the men with me were the only ones who had escaped utter doom.

I begged again that he would deal with us as just men deal with strangers and suppliants, but he, without saying a word, laid hands upon two of my men, and swinging them by the legs, dashed their brains out on the earth. He cut them to pieces and ate them before our very eyes. We wept and we prayed to Zeus as we witnessed a deed so terrible.

Next the Cyclops stretched himself amongst his sheep and went to sleep beside the fire. Then I debated whether I should take my sharp sword in my hand, and feeling where his heart was, stab him there. But second thoughts held me back from doing this. I might be able to kill him as he slept, but not even with my companions could I roll away the great stone that closed the mouth of the cave.

Dawn came, and the Cyclops awakened, kindled his fire and milked his flocks. Then he seized two others of my men and made ready for his midday meal. And now he rolled away the great stone and drove his flocks out of the cave.

I had pondered on a way of escape, and I had thought of something that might be done to baffle the Cyclops. I had with me a great skin of sweet wine, and I thought that if I could make him drunken with wine I and my companions might be able for him. But there were other preparations to be made first. On the floor of the cave there was a great beam of olive wood which the Cyclops had cut to make a club when the wood should be seasoned. It was yet green. I and my companions went and cut off a fathom's length of the wood, and sharpened it to a point and took it to the fire and hardened it in the glow. Then I hid the beam in a recess of the cave.

The Cyclops came back in the evening, and opening up the cave drove in his flocks. Then he closed the cave again with the stone and went and milked his ewes and his goats. Again he seized two of my companions. I went to the terrible creature with a bowl of wine in my hands. He took it and drank it and cried out, 'Give me another bowl of this, and tell me thy name that I may give thee gifts for bringing me this honey-tasting drink.'

Again I spoke to him guilefully and said, 'Noman is my name. Noman my father and my mother call me.'

'Give me more of the drink, Noman,' he shouted. 'And the gift that I shall give to thee is that I shall make thee the last of thy fellows to be eaten.'

I gave him wine again, and when he had taken the third bowl he sank backwards with his face upturned, and sleep came upon him. Then I, with four companions, took that beam of olive wood, now made into a hard and pointed stake,and thrust it into the ashes of the fire. When the pointed end began to glow we drew it out of the flame. Then I and my companions laid hold on the great stake and, dashing at the Cyclops, thrust it into his eye. He raised a terrible cry that made the rocks ring, and we dashed away into the recesses of the cave.

His cries brought other Cyclopes to the mouth of the cave, and they, naming him as Polyphemus, called out and asked him what ailed him to cry. 'Noman,' he shrieked out, 'Noman is slaying me by guile.' They answered him saying, 'If no man is slaying thee, there is nothing we can do for thee, Polyphemus. What ails thee has been sent to thee by the gods.' Saying this, they went away from the mouth of the cave without attempting to move away the stone.

Polyphemus then, groaning with pain, rolled away the stone and sat before the mouth of the cave with his hands outstretched, thinking that he would catch us as we dashed out. I showed my companions how we might pass by him. I laid hands on certain rams of the flock and I lashed three of them together with supple rods. Then on the middle ram I put a man of my company. Thus every three rams carried a man. As soon as the dawn had come the rams hastened out to the pasture, and, as they passed, Polyphemus laid hands on the first and the third of each three that went by. They passed out and Polyphemus did not guess that a ram that he did not touch carried out a man.

For myself, I took a ram that was the strongest and fleeciest of the whole flock and I placed myself under him, clinging to the wool of his belly. As this ram, the best of all his flock, went by, Polyphemus, laying his hands upon him, said, 'Would that you, the best of my flock, were endowed with speech, so that you might tell me where Noman, who has blinded me, has hidden himself.' The ram went by him, and when he had gone a little way from the cave I loosed myself from him and went and set my companions free.

We gathered together many of Polyphemus' sheep and we drove them down to our ship. The men we had left behind would have wept when they heard what had happened to six of their companions. But I bade them take on board the sheep we had brought and pull the ship away from that land. Then when we had drawn a certain distance from the shore I could not forbear to shout my taunts into the cave of Polyphemus. 'Cyclops,' I cried, 'you thought that you had the people of a fool and a weakling to eat. But you have been worsted by me, and your evil deeds have been punished.'

So I shouted, and Polyphemus came to the mouth of the cave with great anger in his heart. He took up rocks and cast them at the ship and they fell before the prow. The men bent to the oars and pulled the ship away or it would have been broken by the rocks he cast. And when we were further away I shouted to him:

'Cyclops, if any man should ask who it was set his mark upon you, say that he was Odysseus, the son of Laertes.'

Then I heard Polyphemus cry out, 'I call upon Poseidon, the god of the sea, whose son I am, to avenge me upon you, Odysseus. I call upon Poseidon to grant that you, Odysseus, may never come to your home, or if the gods have ordained your return, that you come to it after much toil and suffering, in an evil plight and in a stranger's ship, to find sorrow in your home.'

So Polyphemus prayed and, to my evil fortune, Poseidon heard his prayer. But we went on in our ship, rejoicing at our escape. We came to the waste island where my other ships were. All the company rejoiced to see us, although they had to mourn for their six companions slain by Polyphemus. We divided amongst the ships the sheep we had taken from Polyphemus' flock and we sacrificed to the gods. At the dawn of the next day we raised the sails on each ship and we sailed away."

II. Circe

"After we left the island of the cannibal, we sailed on to divers places, always turning wearily to the homes we longed to see, and always barred from sailing there by the enmity of great Poseidon the World-girdler, the Lord of Horses. In our weary exile we came at last to the island of Circe [*SIR-see*] the Enchantress.

"For two days and two nights we were on that island without seeing the sign of a habitation. On the third day I saw smoke rising up from some hearth. I spoke of it to my men, and it seemed good to us that part of our company should go to see were there people there who might help us. We drew lots to find out who should go, and it fell to the lot of Eurylochus to go with part of the company, while I remained with the other part.

So Eurylochus went with two and twenty men. In the forest glades they came upon a house built of polished stones. All round that house wild beasts roamed—wolves and lions. But these beasts were not fierce. As Eurylochus and his men went toward the house, the lions and wolves fawned upon them like house dogs.

But the men were affrighted and stood round the outer gate of the court. They heard a voice within the house singing, and it seemed to them to be the voice of a woman, singing as she went to and fro before a web she was weaving on a loom. The men shouted, and she who had been singing opened the polished doors and came out of the dwelling. She was very fair to see. As she opened the doors of the house she asked the men to come within and they went into her halls.

But Eurylochus tarried behind. He watched the woman and he saw her give food to the men. But he saw that she mixed a drug with what she gave them to eat and with the wine she gave them to drink. No sooner had they eaten the food and drunk the wine than she struck them with a wand, and behold! The men turned into swine. Then the woman drove them out of the house and put them in the swinepens and gave them acorns and mast and the fruit of the cornel tree to eat.

Eurylochus, when he saw these happenings, ran back through the forest and told me all. Then I cast about my shoulder my good sword of bronze, and, bidding Eurylochus stay by the ships, I went through the forest and came to the house of the Enchantress. I stood at the outer court and called out. Then Circe the Enchantress flung wide the shining doors, and called to me to come within. I entered her dwelling and she brought me to a chair and put a footstool under my feet. Then she brought me in a golden cup the wine into which she had cast a harmful drug.

As she handed me the cup I drew my sword and sprang at her as one eager to slay her. She shrank back from me and cried out, 'Who art thou who art able to guess at my enchantments? Verily, thou art Odysseus, of whom Hermes told me. Nay, put up thy sword and let us two be friendly to each other. In all things I will treat thee kindly.'

But I said to her, 'Nay, Circe, you must swear to me first that thou wilt not treat me guilefully.'

She swore by the gods that she would not treat me guilefully, and I put up my sword. Then the handmaidens of Circe prepared a bath, and I bathed and rubbed myself with olive oil, and Circe gave me a new mantle and doublet. The handmaidens brought out silver tables, and on them set golden baskets with bread and meat in them, and others brought cups of honey-tasting wine. I sat before a silver table but I had no pleasure in the food before me.

When Circe saw me sitting silent and troubled she said, 'Why, Odysseus, dost thou sit like a speechless man? Dost thou think there is a drug in this food? But I have sworn that I will not treat thee guilefully, and that oath I shall keep.'

And I said to her, 'O Circe, Enchantress, what man of good heart

could take meat and drink while his companions are as swine in swinepens? If thou wouldst have me eat and drink, first let me see my companions in their own forms.'

Circe, when she heard me say this, went to the swinepen and anointed each of the swine that was there with a charm. As she did, the bristles dropped away and the limbs of the man were seen. My companions became men again, and were even taller and handsomer than they had been before.

After that we lived on Circe's island in friendship with the Enchantress. She did not treat us guilefully again, and we feasted in her house for a year."

III. The Further Voyage

"But a man longs for his own land. At last, I asked Circe for her leave to sail away, and graciously she feasted us upon the beach by our swift ship.

"When the sun sank and darkness came on, my men went to lie by the hawsers of the ship. Then Circe the Enchantress took my hand, and, making me sit down by her, told me of the voyage that was before us.

'To the Sirens first you shall come,' said she, 'to the Sirens, who sit in their field of flowers and bewitch all men who come near them. He who comes near the Sirens without knowing their ways and hears the sound of their voices—never again shall that man see wife or child, or have joy of his home-coming. All round where the Sirens sit are great heaps of the bones of men. But I will tell thee, Odysseus, how thou mayst pass them.'

'When thou comest near put wax over the ears of thy company lest any of them hear the Sirens' song. But if thou thyself art minded to hear, let thy company bind thee hand and foot to the mast. And if thou shalt beseech them to loose thee, then must they bind thee with tighter bonds. When thy companions have driven the ship past where the Sirens sing then thou canst be unbound.'

'Past where the Sirens sit there is a dangerous place indeed. On one side there are great rocks which the gods call the Rocks Wandering. No ship ever escapes that goes that way. And round these rocks the planks of ships and the bodies of men are tossed by waves of the sea and storms of fire. One ship only ever passed that way, Jason's ship, the *Argo*, and that ship would have been broken on the rocks if Hera the goddess had not helped it to pass because of her love for the hero Jason.'

'On the other side of the Rocks Wandering are two peaks through which thou wilt have to take thy ship. One peak is smooth and sheer and goes up to the clouds of heaven. In the middle of it there is a cave, and that cave is the den of a monster named Scylla. This monster has six necks and on each neck there is a hideous head. She holds her heads over the gulf, seeking for prey and yelping horribly. No ship has ever passed that way without Scylla seizing and carrying off in each mouth of her six heads the body of a man.'

'The other peak is near. Thou couldst send an arrow across to it from Scylla's den. Out of the peak a fig tree grows, and below that fig tree Charybdis has her den. She sits there sucking down the water and spouting it forth. Mayst thou not be near when she sucks the water down, for then nothing could save thee. Keep nearer to Scylla's than to Charybdis' rock. It is better to lose six of your company than to lose thy ship and all thy company. Keep near Scylla's rock and drive right on.'

'If thou shouldst win past the deadly rocks guarded by Scylla and Charybdis thou wilt come to the Island of Thrinacia. There the Cattle of the Sun graze with immortal nymphs to guard them. If thou comest to that Island, do no hurt to those herds. If thou doest hurt to them I forsee ruin for thy ship and thy men, even though thou thyself shouldst escape.'

So Circe spoke to me, and having told me such things she took her way up the island. Then I went to the ship and roused my men. Speedily they went aboard, and, having taken their seats upon the benches, struck the water with their oars. Then the sails were hoisted and a breeze came and we sailed away from the Isle of Circe, the Enchantress."

"Everything came to be as the Enchantress had foretold it. Such was the beauty of the song the Sirens made that I twisted in my bonds until the blood dripped from my hands, so eagerly did I strive in my foolishness to throw myself upon the mercies of those pitiless creatures. Then we came to the course between Scylla and Charybdis. Mindful of what Circe said, I hugged the shore close by the cave of Scylla, thinking I could stand armed upon the deck and drive away the monster. Alas for anyone who thinks he can outwit the powerful gods! For in an instant she had seized six of my best men from off the deck and taken them back to her cave to devour them at leisure. They cried to me to save them, but I could only urge us quickly past, and soon they ceased to cry out. Of all the dreadful things that I have seen, that sight was the most pitiful.

Then we reached Thrinacia, that beautiful island where the Titan who guides the Sun pastures his wondrous cattle. From Poseidon's wrath there was no escape, for we were stormbound on that island till we were faint with hunger, and as I slept my men took wicked counsel, and slew the sacred animals to feast themselves. With heavy heart we sailed away at last, until Zeus destroyed us in a sudden storm, and I alone survived.

I was cast up from the bitter sea upon the island where the nymph Calypso keeps her home, and for seven years she made me her unwilling husband, while every day I sought the shore to salt my eyes with bitter longing for my homeland. For nothing is dearer to a man than his homeland, where he can kiss his wife and children, and see again his aged parents. Finally the goddess helped me sail away, until Poseidon struck the sea in wrath again before me and I was cast naked onto your shores."

After listening to his story, the Phaeacians loaded Odysseus with presents and sent him home at last to Ithaca. There he found himself a stranger in his own house. The young men, the ones too young to fight at Troy, had moved in, seeking to take over his property and marry his queen, Penelope. Whoever married her would become king; and since they believed Odysseus would never return, they demanded she choose among them. But Penelope found ways of putting them off. . . .

And then Odysseus returned. How he dealt with the suitors, set his house in order, and was reunited with Penelope and his son Telemachus, who was only an infant when he sailed away, is the subject of the final books of *The Odyssey*.

JOURNEYS TO
THE OTHER WORLD

In the myths there are many worlds. Gods and other powerful beings have realms which they alone inhabit. They may join humans on earth from time to time, but the ways of the gods are not the ways of women and men. The dead, too, have their own world, and both gods and people may grieve when someone dear to them is taken to that other place.

There are many myths about attempts by inhabitants of one world to reach another. Sometimes the journey ends in success or compromise. Often travelers must accept the reality that the two worlds are separate, and that they may not have the power to choose which world they or those they love will inhabit.

Whether these myths are about gods and goddesses or men and women, the feelings in them are very human. They once again remind us that one of the basic impulses in myth is the need to understand the mysteries of life and the world we live in.

The Death of Balder

BY DOROTHY HOSFORD

Loki the trickster has a dark side, too. One day he does a deed for which the gods cannot forgive him.

B alder was the fairest and most beloved of all the gods. He was wise in judgment, gracious in speech, and all his deeds were pure and good. Wherever Balder went there was joy and warmth and gladness. He was beloved by gods and men, and so beautiful that the whitest flower which grew on the hillside was named "Balder's Brow."

It came about that Balder dreamed great and perilous dreams touching his life. Night after night they troubled his sleep. When Balder spoke of these dreams to the other gods, they were filled with foreboding. They knew some danger threatened him, and all the gods took counsel together as to how they might save Balder. They came to this decision: they would ask safety for Balder from every kind of danger.

Frigg, who was the mother of Balder, went to all things in the world to ask their help. Fire and water, stones, earth, and trees, iron and metal of all kinds, birds, beasts, and even serpents promised they would not harm Balder.

When the gods knew that Balder was safe, they made up a game which they took delight in playing. Balder would stand in a circle of the gods and they would strike at him or hurl stones or cast missiles of one kind or another. But Balder stood unhurt in the midst of it all. And this seemed to the gods a wondrous thing, full of awe.

Loki alone was not pleased that Balder took no hurt. His evil, crafty mind began to plot against Balder the Good. Loki made himself appear like an old woman, and in this likeness he went to the dwelling of Balder's mother. He greeted Frigg and she asked him if he knew what the gods were doing at their assembly.

"The gods have a new game. Balder stands before them and they hurl weapons of every kind at him," answered Loki, speaking with the voice of an old woman. "It is a strange thing that nothing harms him."

"Nothing will harm Balder, neither weapons nor rocks nor trees," said Frigg. "I have taken oaths of them all."

"Have all things taken oaths to spare Balder?" asked the old woman.

"All things save one," said Frigg. "A small tree-sprout grows west of Valhalla. It is called Mistletoe. I thought it too young a thing to be bound by an oath."

Immediately the old woman went away. Loki changed himself into his own shape and went west of Valhalla. He tore up the Mistletoe by the roots and carried it to where the gods were assembled.

Hod, the brother of Balder, took no part in the game because he was blind. He stood outside the ring of men.

Loki spoke to him. "Why do you not shoot at Balder?"

"I cannot see where Balder stands, nor have I any weapons," answered Hod.

Then Loki said: "You should do as the others do and show Balder honor. I will show you where he stands. Shoot at him with this wand."

Hod took the Mistletoe wand and shot at Balder, and Loki guided his hand.

The shaft flew through Balder and he fell dead to the earth. This was the greatest mischance that had ever befallen gods and men.

When Balder fell to the earth, the gods could not speak a word for grief and anguish, nor could they move to lift him where he lay. Each looked at the other and they were all of one mind whose evil hand had done this deed. Yet they could take no revenge for they stood on hallowed ground.

When they tried to speak, the tears came and the gods wept bitterly for the loss of Balder. They had no words with which to name their sorrow. Of them all Odin grieved most, for he understood best how great was the loss which had come to the gods.

The mother of Balder was the first to speak. "If any among you," said Frigg, "would win all my love and favor, let him ride the road to Hela's realm and seek Balder among the dead. Let him offer Hela a ransom if she will but let Balder come home to Asgard."

Hermod the Bold undertook the perilous journey. The great eight-footed horse of Odin, named Sleipnir, was brought forth. Hermod mounted and sped at once upon his way.

The gods took the body of Balder and brought it down to the sea, where Balder's ship was drawn up upon the shore. The gods wished to launch the ship and build Balder's funeral pyre upon it, but they could not move it from its place.

Then Odin sent for the giantess Hyrrokin, famed for her strength. She thrust the boat into the waters with such might that fire burst from the rollers beneath and the earth trembled.

When the funeral pyre had been built, the body of Balder was borne to the ship. When his wife, Nanna, saw it her heart broke with grief and she died. The gods, with sorrow, laid her body beside Balder. The fire was kindled. Thor stood near. With a sad heart he lifted his hammer above the blaze and hallowed the flames.

People of many races came to the burning. First of all was Odin. His two ravens flew above him and Frigg was by his side. The Valkyries were also with him. Frey rode in his chariot drawn by his boar called Gold-Mane, and Freya drove her cats. Then came the other gods and goddesses. Many from the lands of the Frost-Giants and the Hill-Giants were there also. All grieved for Balder.

Odin laid upon the fire his ring which was called Draupnir, from which every ninth night dropped eight gold rings like to itself. The flames from the funeral ship rose on high, shining in the air and on the waters. The hearts of the gods were heavy with grief as they watched the burning.

Meanwhile Hermod was on his way to Hela. He rode nine nights through valleys so dark and deep that he could see nothing. At length he came to the river Gjoll. He rode on to the bridge which is paved with glittering gold and guarded by the maiden Modgud. She asked Hermod his name and from what country and people he came.

"Only yesterday," she said, "five companies of dead men crossed this bridge. But today it thunders as much under you riding alone. Nor have you the pallor of death. Why come you this way?"

"I have been sent to seek Balder among the dead," Hermod answered. "Has Balder passed this road?"

The maiden answered that Balder had crossed the bridge. "The way lies downward and to the north," she said.

Hermod rode on until he came to the wall of Hela's realm. He got down from his horse and made the girths of the saddle tight. Then he mounted again and pricked the horse with his spurs. In one great leap Sleipnir cleared the gates.

Hermod rode to the great hall where the dead were gathered. He dismounted and went inside. There he saw Balder sitting in the place of honor. Hermod stayed through the night. When morning came, he begged Hela that Balder might ride home with him.

"The gods are desolate without him," said Hermod. "Every being in the world longs for his return."

Hela answered that it should be put to a test whether Balder were so greatly beloved.

"If all things in the world, living and dead, weep for him," said Hela, "he shall go back to Asgard and the gods. But if there is one thing which bears him no love and will not weep, Balder must remain with me."

When Hermod rose to leave, Balder went with him out of the hall. Balder gave the ring Draupnir to Hermod and asked that he take it to Odin for a remembrance. Nanna, Balder's wife, sent Frigg a linen smock and other gifts.

Hermod rode back and came to Asgard. He told all that he had seen and heard. Then the gods sent messengers all over the world to ask all things to weep for Balder, that he might return to them. All wept for Balder: men, and all living things; the earth and stones and trees, and every kind of metal. In the early morning you can still see their tears when the dew lies upon the grass.

As the messengers came home, their work well done, they found an old woman sitting by a cave. They asked her, as they had asked all others, to weep tears that Balder might come forth from the place of the dead. But she answered:

"I will weep no tears for Balder. I loved him not. Let Hela keep what she holds. Let her keep what she holds."

And because one out of all the world would not weep for the god, Balder must stay where he was. Gods and men knew that this again was

Loki's evil work. This time he must pay the price for all that he had done. The gods revenged themselves on Loki. But Balder remained with Hela, and the earth was never again as fair to gods or men.

The Children of Loki

For this deed the gods could not forgive Loki. They bound him beneath the earth in chains that will not be broken until the last day, when the powers of destruction, led by Loki and his children, will break loose and rise against the gods.

For Loki had children born in Myrkwood, the Dark Wood, who were the greatest of monsters and the worst enemies of the gods. The eldest child was a monstrous serpent, whom Odin hurled into the sea surrounding Midgard, the Middle Earth where we live. Here he became so vast he circles the world, biting on his tail. The second child was the giant wolf, Fenris, the power of ravening destruction, whom the gods could only bind with a magic chain made for them by the dwarves. The third child was Hela.

On the last day, Thor will meet the Midgard Serpent again, and each will destroy the other. Odin himself will be devoured by the Fenris wolf, and in the general war all of earth and heaven will be overwhelmed by fire. The Norse called this final battle *Ragnarok*. The German word is *Götterdammerung*, usually translated as "Twilight of the Gods." It is known that Hitler was obsessed with this idea, and perhaps his deepest wish was not to win the Second World War, but to overwhelm the earth in destruction.

In the myth, though, the end of the gods is not the end. A new dawn will come, with a new sun and moon, and a new green earth. Out from their hiding place a new woman and a new man will come, to found a new human race ruled by kinder passions, and Balder will return from the land of death to rule over earth and heaven.

Demeter and Persephone

BY CELIA BARKER LOTTRIDGE

This is a myth about the balance between life and death, and how compromise keeps our earth in order.

D emeter was the goddess who loved the earth. While most of the gods spent their days on Mount Olympus in the company of other gods, Demeter loved to wander the fields and forests, visiting the country people who offered her hospitality. They knew that the simply-dressed woman with the golden eyes and golden hair must be one of the immortals, because of the nobility of her bearing and the wisdom in her face.

She had a daughter who was her heart's joy. As Demeter loved the fields of grain and the trees laden with fruit, so her daughter Persephone loved flowers and the spring time. Her step was light and her smile was like sunshine.

Hades, lord of the underworld, saw Persephone and fell in love with her. Although his palace was built of gold and its walls were rich with precious stones, it was dark and gloomy. Hades longed for the brightness and joy that Persephone would bring to his kingdom, so he went to Zeus and asked for her as his bride. Zeus did not want to offend his older brother, but he knew that Demeter would never agree to send her daughter to the underworld. So if he did not forbid Hades to marry Persephone, he did not approve of it, either. Hades saw that Zeus would not stand against him, so he proceeded with his plan.

Persephone was gathering flowers in a meadow one day when a

golden chariot drawn by four coal-black horses burst through a crevasse in the earth. The driver of the chariot grasped the girl by her wrist and pulled her into the chariot beside him, before he turned his horses and plunged again into the earth. Only a few crushed blossoms remained to show that Persephone had been there.

When Demeter came looking for her daughter, of course she could not find her. For nine days she wandered, asking all she met if they had seen Persephone. At last, a story told by a country man gave her the dreadful suspicion that her beloved daughter had been taken into the underworld. She went to Helios the sun, who sees everything, and demanded to hear the truth.

When Helios told her that Persephone had been taken by Hades to be his queen, Demeter's anger knew no bounds. She left Olympus and walked barefoot on the earth, her hair disheveled, mourning her loss. And the earth, which had been so dear to her, became desolate. The goddess forbade the fields and the trees to bear. Streams dried up; and dust blew in the hot wind. Ploughs could not cut the fields, and seeds that were scattered did not grow. People began to starve; and the beloved goddess who had been their friend walked among them unrecognized, for her eyes were blank, her gown tattered, and her body bent with grief.

Zeus sent one god after another to plead with her, but Demeter would not hear any of them. "Until my daughter is returned to me, the earth will show the sorrow in my heart," she said.

Zeus, the Father of Heaven, knew he could not let the earth die. He also knew that Persephone, the eternally young, did not belong in the underworld. So he called Hermes, the messenger of the gods, who guides the souls of the dead to their new home, and said, "Go to Hades. Tell him that he must allow Persephone to return to Demeter. He must let her go— unless she has eaten any of the food of the dead. If she has done that, she must remain below the earth."

And so Hermes found Hades sitting on his gloomy throne and told him what Zeus had said. Hades knew he had no choice and he called for Persephone, his queen. She came with her head bent and her steps dragging; but Hermes saw that even in her misery she brought brightness and warmth to that cold metal palace, and he knew why Hades wanted her.

When Persephone heard that Hermes had come to take her away from there, her eyes brightened and color came into her pale cheeks. But

Hades said, "If you have eaten anything during your time here you cannot leave, for no one can eat the food of the dead and return to live on earth." Persephone said nothing; but as she left Hades' palace one of the gardeners cried out that he had seen her eat four seeds from a pomegranate, the fruit of the dead.

Demeter greeted her daughter with great joy, and in all the desolate world the sap began to rise again. But Persephone confessed that she had indeed eaten the pomegranate seeds, and that Hades would finally claim her. Then Zeus saw that he must act to stop death from overtaking the earth. Equally, the old days of endless spring and summer could be no more.

He spoke to both Demeter and Hades. "Because Persephone ate four seeds in the underworld, she will spend four months of the year with Hades. But always she will return to her mother Demeter to bring flowers and brightness to the earth." And Demeter and Hades and Persephone knew that this was the way it would be.

Demeter sorrowed that Persephone would be in a world so far from the light for so long each year. But now her sorrow did not overwhelm her. She looked at the dry, barren earth and the golden light of love came into her eyes once more. She began to walk the fields and groves again, and again they flourished.

The Journey of Gilgamesh

BY BERNARDA BRYSON

Gilgamesh may be the oldest written story to come down to us. It was first told by the Sumerians, an ancient people of the land we now call Iraq, as early as 3000 B.C. In the thousands of years that followed, it was recorded on clay tablets in a wedge-shaped script called cuneiform. These tablets, found in the ruins of ancient cities, have been deciphered.

Gilgamesh was the King of Uruk, the most splendid of the seven cities of Sumer. Like many ancient kings he was part god, part human, and was thus stronger than the ordinary people of his city. Uruk was renowned for the high walls that protected it from enemy armies, wild animals, and monsters, and Gilgamesh ordered the people of the city to build these walls higher and still higher. At last the people of Uruk were wearied by the labor Gilgamesh commanded them to do, and they appealed to the gods. The gods created a wild man called Enkidu to fight the king and distract him from his wall building. But after a mighty battle, Gilgamesh and Enkidu made peace with each other and became like brothers.

Together they fought and destroyed a giant called Humbaba. The goddess Ishtar watched the battle, and she fell in love with Gilgamesh. But Gilgamesh knew that those whom Ishtar loved often suffered miserable fates when she tired of them, and he told the goddess he would not be her husband.

Ishtar's anger was terrible. She made her father, the god Anu, send a monstrous bull to destroy the city of Uruk. But together Gilgamesh and Enkidu killed the bull. Now Ishtar sought a new way to attack Gilgamesh, a way against which he had no defense. She sent death to Enkidu.

Gilgamesh was stricken with grief for his friend, and for the first time he feared his own death. He thought of his ancestor Utnapishtim, who had been given immortality by the gods: perhaps he could tell Gilgamesh the secret of escaping death. But Utnapishtim lived beyond the Bitter River that encircled the world of human beings. No one could cross that river and live, for its very water meant death. But Gilgamesh was determined to try to reach the world beyond the Bitter River.

I. The Scorpion Men

It is not known how many double-hours, that is, how many days and nights Gilgamesh walked. But he crossed deserts and rocky places and came in time to the edge of the world. Before him loomed the mighty mountains of Mashu, and he asked himself, "Can these be the mountains whose peaks reach into the heavens, and whose feet reach below the bottom of the earth? Is this the bank of the sun—the edge between day and night? Is this the mountain guarded by the terrible scorpion men whose radiance blinds one and whose look is death?"

And as he stood questioning himself, he looked upward and saw these men standing above him in the snowy pass; and they sparkled and shone with a bright radiance.

He heard one of the creatures call out to his wife, "Who is this that comes here, is he god or man?"

The wife called back, "Two-thirds of his flesh is the same as that of the gods, but the other third is a man's flesh."

The scorpion man called down to him, cupping his hands, "How is it that you've come here to me, crossing deserts and all sorts of difficult places?"

Gilgamesh shouted back despairingly, "O, I have lost my friend, Enkidu, sir, he who roved the fields and woods with me and was my constant companion. The earth reached up and seized him!"

"But why do you come here to this place?"

"I have come to search for Utnapishtim, my ancestor. He was once a mortal man, but he entered the assembly of the gods. He knows the secret of life and death; I must find out from him where my friend has gone and whether I too must die!"

"O Gilgamesh," said the scorpion man, "no one has ever done this thing. Deep are the caverns that lie under the mountain, those very caverns that the sun travels on his way back to the Eastern Garden. At a distance of nine double-hours only, Gilgamesh, the heart fails. Dense is the darkness; there is no light! At a distance of ten double-hours, the mind fails! At first, the cold is unbearable, but in the middle part, the heat is unbearable. And although the whole distance is only that of twelve double-hours, it is the same distance as that between life and death! Turn back, Gilgamesh!"

But Gilgamesh replied, "Even if my heart fails, I will go on! In heat or cold I will go on. Sighing or weeping I will go on!"

The scorpion man was silent for a time, but when he spoke he said, "Go, Gilgamesh! I will open the gates for you. May your feet carry you in safety!"

As the gates of rock swung open Gilgamesh entered into the earth and followed the way of the sun. Darkness closed around him; he could not see what lay ahead of him or what way he had come. The path was strewn with rocks and he stumbled often. At first his body shook with cold, but as he descended more and more deeply into the earth, heat surrounded him, and he sweat and panted for breath. Sometimes he seemed to have been walking only a short way, but at other times he felt that he had been trudging his life out in the darkness. There was no sound there other than the unceasing scraping of his own feet as he felt his way along.

He strained his eyes to see, but it was as though they were closed. There was nothing, no trace of light. Could the caverns be endless? Had the scorpion man only trapped him, and was he now laughing at him, high up in the mountain pass?

At a distance of nine double-hours Gilgamesh's heart failed him and he was full of terror. At a distance of ten double-hours his mind failed him. He opened his mouth and shouted with all his might, and the echoes of his own voice swarmed back all around him, terrible to hear. He began to run, but he stumbled and fell.

So Gilgamesh lay in the darkness and could no longer cry out. He closed his eyes; he could not get up or turn backward or go forward. And then he felt the wind from the north blowing upon his face.

He rose and stumbled on in the black place. At a distance of eleven double-hours he perceived a trace of light and his eyes filled with tears of joy. At a distance of twelve double-hours he emerged from the cavern and stood in the Eastern Garden.

All around him rose trees that sparkled with precious gems. Water glittered in fountains and in pools; the air was full of sweet smells, and flowers of every kind nodded in the breeze. Here was such a light as he had never seen. "Can this be the Eastern Garden, called Dilmun, the most beautiful of places?" As Gilgamesh wondered, he looked through the trees into the huge face of Shamash, the sun.

Shamash came to him, greeting him, and Gilgamesh called out to him, "O great Shamash, the darkness has gone from my eyes! Let me only gaze at you! Let me look at you and be filled with your light!"

"What are you doing here, my son?" asked Shamash. "How have you come here? Why are you dressed in the rough skins of animals? Why are your looks so wild, your face burned, your body so thin and emaciated?"

"I have lost my friend and brother Enkidu! The earth came up and seized him, and since that time I have known no rest. Now, O great Shamash, I am on my way to find my ancestor who was chosen a long time ago to live among the immortals. From him I shall learn the secret of life and death; I will preserve life!"

"Why do you run hither and thither, Gilgamesh? The life you seek you will never find!"

"Tell me," said Gilgamesh, "shall the one who has died rest his head forever underneath the earth? Shall he sleep for all the years and never see your light, O Shamash? And shall I too die?"

"Why should you waste your young years this way, my son? Stay here beside me! Live in this garden where there is no grief and no memory!"

But Gilgamesh would not rest or remain in the garden. "In your travels across the sky, great Shamash, you must see all things! Tell me then how to find my ancestor in the place of the immortals."

Shamash pointed to a path that led downward through the jeweled trees. "In that direction you will find Sabitu, the wine maiden. She will tell you the way to go. But remember, Gilgamesh, what you seek has never been." And so speaking, Shamash gathered his glorious robes about him and ascended into the sky.

II. Sabitu

The maiden Sabitu was in front of her house tending her casks of wine. Hearing footsteps, she looked up and saw the wild countenance of Gilgamesh. She ran into her house and bolted the door. "Surely some murderer has made his way here—some savage!"

But Gilgamesh knocked and pleaded with her to open her door. "I am Gilgamesh, King of distant Uruk! Talk to me, O Sabitu, tell me what I want to know!"

Sabitu was overcome by curiosity. "If you are a king, why are you dressed in the skins of wild animals? Why is your face burned as though you had walked through a furnace? Why are you wan and unkempt like a wild man?"

When Gilgamesh told her of his grief and his fearful journey beneath the earth, the maiden was moved by pity. She came out of her house and invited him to sit on a bench beside her. She brought him wine and meat and fruits, and comforted him with kind words.

"But where are you going, Gilgamesh?"

"I am on my way to find my ancestor, Utnapishtim. He lives somewhere among the immortals; from him I shall learn the secret of life and death!"

"Ah, whither do you run, Gilgamesh? The life you seek you will never find!"

"Only tell me the path, Sabitu. If it is a sea that I must cross, then I will cross it; but if not, then I will walk over the desert and the wild steppes, but still I will find Utnapishtim!"

"Deep are the waters, Gilgamesh! Whoever has come even so far as this place has never yet made the crossing. For ahead of you now lies the Bitter River whose waters are death. When you come to the edge of the water, what will you do?"

And she went on, saying, "Listen to me, Gilgamesh; when the gods created mankind they allotted death to mankind, but life they retained in their own keeping! Rest here, O King! Let your garments be clean and your headband made of gold! Be glad; let your belly be full! Drink the good sesame wine and make every day a day of rejoicing! Take a wife to your bosom; such is the life the gods allotted to mankind!"

Gilgamesh thanked her. "I must go on, O Sabitu. Tell me which way I must take."

Sabitu led Gilgamesh by his hand to the edge of her garden. She pointed toward a vast plain of dark and dismal water, edged by a white shore. "That way, O King, lies the Bitter River. On the shore you will find an ancient boat and the pilot, Urshanabi. Only he can take you across, but no living man has ever sat beside him!" She wished him well and returned to her vineyard.

III. How Gilgamesh Crossed the Bitter River

Thus Gilgamesh came to the Bitter River. He looked out across its water and up and down the shore, but nowhere could he see either boat or boatman. He walked farther and after some distance he espied a boat and went to it. Still there was no person nearby. He called; he cupped his hands and shouted but there was no answer. He sat down beside the boat and waited—he could not tell how long, for there was neither day nor night by which to measure the time. He was impatient; he searched; he called continually and there was no reply.

Raging, Gilgamesh picked up a huge rock and with it he smashed the stone oarlocks of the boat. Indeed, he might have destroyed the boat itself, but he heard a voice shouting at him: "Hello, there! What are you doing? Who are you who dares to lay hands on the boat of Utnapishtim?"

Utnapishtim! Gilgamesh cursed his impatience and his rage. "O, I am weary, boatman! I have come far. I have crossed the Mountains of Mashu and walked under the foundation of the earth! In heat and cold I have come! Sighing and weeping I have come ever onward, to seek my ancestor Utnapishtim! Forgive my rage, O boatman; forgive my anger, for I've grown impatient. Only take me across this water to the place of Utnapishtim!"

The boatman shook his head. "No living being has ever crossed these waters, young man. But even if I were willing to ferry you over, it's you who have made that impossible for you have destroyed the oarlocks of the boat."

Gilgamesh felt shame and bowed his head. Then the boatman spoke softly, "Broad is the water, O Wanderer, but if it is your will to cross, then you must do as I say: you must enter the forest and there you must cut and hew one hundred and ten straight poles measuring sixty cubits each. With these we will pole our way across the river. Each pole, once it has reached its length, must be thrown away, for if even so much as a drop of water enters the boat or touches your flesh, you will die."

Urshanabi the boatman then lay down on the beach to sleep while Gilgamesh went into the forest to cut the poles. And when this labor was finished he pulled them to the boat and laid them along its length. And all this done, they set out across the width of the Bitter River.

IV. Utnapishtim

Utnapishtim was lying in his hammock before the door of his house. He called to his wife, saying, "I see the boat approaching across the water, but the boatman is not alone; someone is with him. Come and tell me who it is that rides in the boat with Urshanabi!"

His wife came out of the house and shaded her eyes, looking across the water. "It is a young man not different from you and me, but his body is thin and his looks are wan!"

The boat came to rest beside the quay, and Gilgamesh leapt out and approached Utnapishtim, his ancestor. He fell to his knees and looked at him. "O Utnapishtim, I gaze upon you, and your face is not different from mine! I had thought to find you a dreadful warrior, towering and tall, but here you are lying on your side in your hammock like any mortal man!"

"I am not like you at all!" shouted Utnapishtim. "Look at you, unkempt and woebegone, and dressed in the filthy hides of wild animals! Who are you and how did you get here?"

"I am Gilgamesh, King of Uruk, O Utnapishtim, and you are my ancestor. I have come far through deserts and over wild steppes and under the very foundation of the earth to find you and to ask you a question...."

"You have no right to come here, you a mortal man. The boatman shall be punished!"

"Listen to me, O Utnapishtim! I had a friend dearer to me than a brother. Day and night we went together; together we roamed over the wild steppes and through the forests, hunting and wrestling with wild animals. Together we demolished the monster Humbaba that daily threatened our city; together we killed the Bull of Heaven that had been sent against us to destroy us. Everywhere we walked together, sharing all dangers and all delights. Then death came to Enkidu: the fate of mortal men overtook him! He did not die in battle like some hero; he didn't die of illness or venerable old age; the earth came up and seized him! Then, O Utnapishtim, I was overcome by terror and by grief. Alone, I set out over the wild places of the earth to find you, my ancestor. For I have been told that you were chosen to join the assembly of the gods, and that you know the secret of life and death. Tell me now, O Utnapishtim, must my brother remain for all the years lying at the centre of the earth? Will he never again see the face of the sun, and must I too die?"

Utnapishtim spoke, answering Gilgamesh, "Do we build a house to last forever? When the gods gather together, O Gilgamesh, they decree the destinies of men. The days of life they measure out, but the days of death they do not measure!"

"Then tell me, Utnapishtim, what secret do you know? In what way did you come to be placed among the immortals? Were you, like me, two parts god and only one part mortal man?"

"Not at all," said Utnapishtim. "Squat down on your haunches, Gilgamesh, and listen. I will tell you the story; I will reveal to you the secret of my immortality!"

V. The Magic Weed

Utnapishtim then told Gilgamesh the story of how the gods destroyed man with a flood. Only he and his wife survived. In remorse, the gods gave immortality to Utnapishtim: but this will not happen for Gilgamesh. Then Utnapishtim sent Gilgamesh away.

The wife of Utnapishtim scolded him thus: "O husband, the young man has suffered all sorts of pain and hardship only to see you and talk to you. How can you send him off like this? What will you give him from this place so that he may return to his city in honor?"

Utnapishtim called the boat back to the quay. "Gilgamesh, I will tell you something, namely, a secret of the gods. At the bottom of this river there grows a weed. It bears a flower having the fragrance of a rose. Like a rose too, it has a thorny stem that will prick and scratch the hands. Nevertheless, if any mortal can grasp this weed, if he can pluck it and eat some morsel of it, youth will return to him as the spring-time returns to the year! This secret I tell you."

Gilgamesh shouted loud with joy: "Urshanabi, we shall grasp the weed and pull it loose! We will return to Uruk, you and I; we will share the weed among the aged of the city and they will regain their youth and strength. We will call it 'The-Old-Become-Young-Again!'"

"Beware, O Gilgamesh! This is a trap for your wayward heart! The waters of the river are death, and no one may enter them and still live."

"Old men will become strong again! Grandmothers will become maids!"

"Instead, you will be overcome by the bitter water, O King. Come, let the weed stay where it grows!"

"But if I can grasp the weed it will restore my strength and I will live. Take the boat out on the water, Urshanabi, and wait for me."

Gilgamesh stood on the quay and tied heavy stones to his feet. Slowly he entered the river and the stones pulled him down. The water was thick and full of brine and he could not see. But such was the fragrance of the flower that it penetrated everywhere. Gilgamesh was drawn to it; he touched it; he pulled it out by its roots even though it pricked and scratched his hands. He cut the stones from his feet and the water rejected him and threw him to the far shore.

There Urshanabi waited, and they set out across the land and walked for an unknown distance. They crossed mountains; they came to the sacred forest and passed through it and reached the twilight.

They sat down to rest, and tempted by curiosity, they tasted a morsel of the plant. Immediately all weariness dropped from them. "Let's go on," they said to each other. And now, guided by the rising and sinking of the sun, they walked a distance of twenty double-hours.

Finding a fresh spring of water, they decided to rest and sleep. Gilgamesh threw off his tunic, the gift of his ancestor, and bathed himself in the pool. As he stepped out clean and refreshed he saw a serpent at his feet. The creature grasped the magic plant and slithered off through the grass. Gilgamesh pursued it with loud cries and shouts. But the snake entered a hole in the earth and went underground, leaving behind only the old and withered skin that it had dropped in regaining its youth.

Gilgamesh beat his breast; he wrung his hands. "O Urshanabi, for whom have my hands become tired, my cheeks wan? For whom is my blood spent? For a snake! For an earth-prowler! O my magic weed, O my flower! Who will bring them back to me from under the earth? Why didn't I leave them at the quay of the carpenter?"

Sadly, Gilgamesh returned to Uruk, where the people were amazed to see him again. Even then he was not content: he insisted on traveling further, until at last he met Enkidu at the gates of the underworld. Then, at the end of his quest, it was time for Gilgamesh himself to die.

But the people never forgot him.

The Earliest Stories

Gilgamesh is a distant forerunner of Heracles: both have a sky god as a father and are persecuted by a goddess, both dress themselves in the skin of a lion, and both travel to the underworld when they are still alive.

The walls of Uruk are like the Tower of Babel in the Bible. The Eastern Garden is the Garden of Eden. The Bitter River is like the River Styx that borders the underworld, or the icy sea that separates Midgard from Utgard. Utnapishtim is clearly an early version of Noah. In Hebrew the word for "sun" is still *shamash*, and in Arabic it is *shams*.

Eros and Psyche

BY SEAN ARMSTRONG

A love which tries to bridge the gap between gods and mortals leads to difficulty.

Once a king and queen had three daughters. The first two were beautiful enough; but the youngest daughter, Psyche, was so beautiful that as she grew up people said that she surpassed the goddess Aphrodite. This angered Aphrodite, and she sent her son Eros to punish the girl. "Make her fall in love with some conceited fool," she commanded him.

Eros went to do his mother's bidding, first filling two vials at her fountains with the sweet water of desire and the bitter water of repulsion. Finding Psyche sleeping, he poured the bitter water on her eyelids, so that all would be repelled by her; and then a moment later, overcome by love for her himself, he poured the sweet water on her too.

From then on, Psyche found her beauty bittersweet, and her life became unbearable. Men found her so beautiful they were afraid to approach her, so she lived without any coming forward to love her, and even without friends. At last her father and mother sought help from the oracle of Apollo. But Eros, whose love for Psyche had only grown stronger, had also gone to Apollo to ask for his help. And so the oracle replied, "Take Psyche to a high mountain, and leave her there. She is destined to be the bride of a winged serpent, a monster so terrible that even the gods fear him."

Her parents dared not disobey this terrible command, and Psyche was so miserable she did not object, so she was abandoned on the mountain to meet her doom. It was not long, however, before she felt a gentle breeze lift her into the air, wafting her gently to a sunlit meadow spread before a palace of unearthly beauty. Unseen voices bid her enter and refresh herself, and so she did.

Inside was everything needed to furnish comfort and delight, but no other person. Psyche ate some of the delicious food set out, listened to sweet music played by unseen musicians, and waited for the master to appear. Night fell, and darkness, before Psyche felt a presence with her. Suddenly a gentle hand held hers, and she heard a voice full of melody. "Fear not," it said. "I am your husband. In the darkness we will be together, and all things will be for your delight. In daytime, you may have this palace for your own. But you may never look upon my face, because then I must go away from you forever."

So gentle and so passionate was her unseen companion that Psyche knew that this was the lover and husband she had longed for. From then on, he was with her in the night, and always gone by daylight. This happy life went on for many nights and days, but at last Psyche began to be restless for the company of others, and she asked her lover if she could have her sisters visit her. "Beware Psyche, lest their envy destroy our happiness," he warned her, but in the end he agreed.

When her sisters came, blown by the gentle breezes, Psyche proudly led them through the palace, telling them about her new life. As they gazed on the treasures that surrounded Psyche, jealousy overcame them and they asked her many questions about her mysterious husband. At last she had to admit she had never seen him. "Never seen him?" said one sister. "He must be the monster, then, playing with your trust until he decides to devour you." "The only safe thing," said the other, "is to light a lamp and look at the creature in the night, keeping a knife ready to cut his throat while he's asleep."

Psyche protested, shocked at what her sisters said, but she began to have doubts herself. She forgot the joy she always felt in her lover's presence. Why had he forbidden her to look upon him? There must be some terrible reason. She felt she could not trust him. She must see for herself.

That night, when she knew that he was well asleep, she lit a lamp and held it high over the bed. There before her on the pillow, relaxed in sleep, was the beauty of a god, and Psyche knew that it was Eros, god of love himself. She gasped, and leaned forward to brush his hair back from his cheek. A drop of hot oil from the lamp fell on his naked shoulder, and instantly the god awoke.

"Ah, Psyche," he said mournfully. "If you had not done this we could have stayed as we were. Now I must leave you forever. Love cannot live without trust." With that he disappeared, leaving Psyche alone on the bare hillside.

She refused to accept that he was gone forever. Wracked with weeping and remorse, she wandered through the world offering prayers to any god who might help her. But no one wished to make an enemy of Aphrodite, and Psyche saw that there was no help for her in heaven or on earth. At last she came to Aphrodite's temple, and fell into a weary sleep on the stone steps of the sanctuary. When she awoke Aphrodite was before her.

"You pathetic thing," the goddess said spitefully. "how dare you set yourself up as my equal. You want mercy from me?—I have a task or two to set you first." She led Psyche into a great storeroom behind the temple, full of grain for her sacred doves. But all the grain—wheat, millet, barley, sesame seeds, lentils, flax—was jumbled up together. Psyche's task, the goddess told her, was to separate each into its own pile by nightfall.

The task was impossible, so Psyche wept, wondering what she could do. At that moment, she, who had found no compassion in either gods or humans, aroused the pity of the tiniest of creatures. A column of ants appeared, marching across the floor. The room was soon alive with them, sorting and carrying the seeds; and when Aphrodite returned, the task was done.

The goddess was furious. For her next task, Psyche was sent out at dawn to gather an armful of wool from the golden-fleeced sheep that grazed by the river. Now the reeds spoke to Psyche, warning her that the sheep were murderous while the power of the sun increased. "Wait till afternoon," they whispered; "then the sheep are drowsy, and you can gather easily the tufts of wool they've left on the bushes and thistles."

So Psyche did. Again the goddess was in a fury. "You could not have succeeded without the help of others," she cried. "I have another trial. I lost some of my beauty healing the burn you gave my son. Go down to Hades, and beg Persephone for some beauty to fill this box."

This was a sentence of death, for who could go down into Hades and return alive? Psyche walked numbly away from the temple toward a nearby tower. Wearily she climbed up it to the top, intending to jump off: here was the quickest way to Hades. But then a voice spoke beside her, out of the air, telling her how she might fulfil this task too. "Take two coins under your tongue for the dour ferryman Charon," it said. "Take bread soaked in honey for the terrible three-headed dog Cerberus. Throw it to him, and he will let you pass. Do not fear dread Persephone. She will give you what you ask for, but be sure you do not open the box before you give it to Aphrodite."

Thus guided, Psyche found the entrance into Hades, and waited at the icy river Styx for silent Charon to take her across, paying him with a coin. Resolutely she walked deeper into the silent land of the dead, until she stood before the throne of Persephone. The goddess nodded when Psyche made her request, and took the box for a minute.

Dismissed from Persephone's presence, Psyche returned across the dusty fields and recrossed the river to the shore of the living. At the gates of Hades, Cerberus foamed and raged—he allows no one to leave Hades, though all can enter in—but when she threw him the honey sop he snapped it out of the air and moved aside.

In the upper air again, with the stars above her, Psyche gave a great sigh and fell to her knees in thankfulness. Then, weary as she was, she could not resist looking into the box of beauty, for she knew her trials and sorrows had cost her some of her own beauty. "The goddess will not miss a pinch of it," she thought to herself, as she lifted up the lid. But there was nothing in the box, except darkness like smoke that drew her into a heavy sleep.

It was Eros who found her. Aphrodite had locked the door of his chamber, but she could not keep him from flying out the window. His wound was healed, and he longed for Psyche. He touched her with an arrow to awaken her. "O Psyche," he said, "once again your curiosity has brought you into danger. But now the trials are over. By your strength and faithfulness you have won me back." He took her by the hand and drew her up into heaven, before the throne of Zeus. While Psyche stood confused, Eros begged for the gods' indulgence. "Psyche has proved her love for me," he said, "and therefore let her stay in heaven."

Zeus decreed that it be so, and even Aphrodite relented. Psyche became a goddess, to live with Eros forever.

Pyramus and Thisbe

The story of Eros and Psyche has been seen as an allegory of the soul led onward by the power of love—*psyche* is a Greek word meaning "soul," and *eros* means "desire." Another ancient myth about love—it actually dates back to Babylon—is the story of Pyramus and Thisbe. Shakespeare used it in *Romeo and Juliet*, and burlesqued it in the last act of *A Midsummer Night's Dream*.

Pyramus and Thisbe lived in adjoining houses in the city of Babylon. They were forbidden to meet, since their parents had arranged their marriages to others. However, the two fell in love, even though they could only communicate through a crack in the wall between their houses, passing whispers back and forth, and kissing the wall in frustrated tenderness. Finally, they decided to escape and meet outside the city walls.

Thisbe was the first to arrive at the scene, a marble tomb beside a spring, under a mulberry tree heavy with fruit. In the dusk she waited anxiously for Pyramus. But while she waited, a lioness, jaws bloody from its kill, came to drink at the spring. Thisbe ran to hide in the tomb, dropping her cloak as she did so.

Returning from its drink, the lioness picked up the cloak and mauled it, before heading off into the night. When Pyramus arrived a few minutes later, he found the lioness's footprints and the bloodied cloak. He immediately thought that Thisbe had been killed. Frenzied with grief, he seized his sword and killed himself, his blood flowing so richly over the roots of the mulberry tree that its color mounted to the white fruit, staining them a deep purple. A moment later, Thisbe came out of hiding. Finding the dead body of her lover, she killed herself as well.

The grieving parents placed their ashes in one urn, and the gods decreed that the fruit of the mulberry tree would remain purple forever.

The White Stone Canoe

BY HENRY ROWE SCHOOLCRAFT

This is a story about reconciliation.

There was once a very beautiful young girl, who died suddenly on the day she was to have been married to a handsome young man. He was also brave, but his heart was not strong enough to endure this loss. From the hour she was buried, there was no more joy or peace for him. He would often visit the spot where the women had buried her and sit there, dreaming.

Some of his friends thought he should try to forget his sorrow by hunting or by following the warpath. But war and hunting had lost their charms for him. His heart was already dead within him. He pushed aside both his war club and his bow and arrows.

He had heard the old people say there was a path that led to the land of souls, and he made up his mind to follow it. One morning, after having made his preparations for the journey, he picked up his bow and arrows, called to his dog, and started out. He hardly knew which way to go. He was only guided by the tradition that he must go south. As he walked along, he could see at first no change in the face of the country. Forests and hills and valleys and streams had the same look which they wore in his native place. There was snow on the ground, and sometimes it was even piled and matted on the thick trees and bushes. But after a long while it began to diminish, and finally disappeared. The forest took on a more cheerful appearance, the leaves put forth their buds, and before he was aware of the completeness of the change, he found himself surrounded by spring.

He had left behind him the land of snow and ice. The clouds of winter had rolled away from the sky. The air became mild. A pure field of blue was above him. As he went along he saw flowers beside his path and heard the songs of birds. By these signs he knew that he was going the right way, for they agreed with the traditions of his tribe.

At length he spied a path. It led him through a grove, then up a long, high ridge, on the very top of which there stood a lodge. At the door was an old man with white hair, whose eyes, though deeply sunken, had a fiery brilliance. He had a long robe of skins thrown loosely around his shoulders and a staff in his hands.

The young man began to tell his story. But the old chief stopped him before he had spoken ten words. "I have expected you," he said, "and had just risen to welcome you to my lodge. She whom you seek passed here only a few days ago, and being tired from her journey, rested herself here. Enter my lodge and be seated. I will then answer your questions and give you directions for the remainder of your journey."

When this was accomplished, the old chief brought the young man back out through the door of the lodge. "You see yonder lake," said he, "and the wide-stretching blue plains beyond. It is the land of souls. You now stand upon its borders, and my lodge is at the gate of entrance. But you cannot take your body along. Leave it here with your bow and arrows and your dog. You will find them safe on your return."

So saying, he went back into the lodge, and the traveler bounded forward, as if his feet had suddenly been given the power of wings. But all things retained their natural colors and shapes. The woods and leaves, the streams and lakes, were only brighter and more beautiful than before. Animals bounded across his path with a freedom and confidence that seemed to tell him there was no bloodshed here. Birds of beautiful plumage lived in the groves and sported in the waters.

There was one thing, however, that struck him as peculiar. He noticed that he was not stopped by trees or other objects. He seemed to walk directly through them. They were, in fact, merely the souls or shadows of real trees. He became aware that he was in a land of shadows.

When he had traveled half a day's journey, through a country which grew more and more attractive, he came to the banks of a broad lake, in the center of which was a large and beautiful island. He found a canoe of shining white stone tied to the shore. He was now sure that he had followed the right path, for the aged man had told him of this. There were also shining paddles. He immediately got into the canoe and had just taken the paddles in his hands when, to his joy and surprise, he beheld the object of his search in another canoe, exactly like his own in every respect. She had exactly imitated his motions, and they were side by side.

At once they pushed out from the shore and began to cross the lake. Its waves seemed to be rising, and at a distance looked ready to swallow them up. But just as they came to the whitened edge of the first great wave, it seemed to melt away, as if it had been merely a shadow or a reflection. No sooner did they pass through one wreath of foam, however, than another still more threatening rose up. They were in constant fear. Moreover, through the clear water they could see the bones of many men who had perished, strewn on the bottom of the lake.

The Master of Life had decreed that the two of them should pass safely through, for they had both led good lives on earth. But they saw many others struggling and sinking in the waves. There were old men and young men, and women too. Some passed safely through, and some sank. But it was only the little children whose canoes seemed to meet no waves at all. Finally every difficulty was passed, as if in an instant, and they both leaped out onto the happy island.

They felt that the air was food. It strengthened and nourished them. They wandered over the blissful fields, where everything was made to please the eye and the ear. There were no storms. There was no ice, no chilly wind. No one shivered for want of warm clothes. No one suffered from hunger, no one mourned the dead. They saw no graves. They heard of no wars. There was no hunting for animals, for the air itself was food.

Gladly would the young warrior have remained there forever, but he was obliged to go back for his body. He did not see the Master of Life, but he heard his voice in a soft breeze. "Go back," said the voice, "to the land where you came from. Your time has not yet come. The duties for which I made you, and which you are to perform, are not yet finished. Return to your people and accomplish the duties of a good man. You will be the ruler of your tribe for many days. The rules you must observe will be told you by my messenger who keeps the gate. When he gives you back your body, he will tell you what to do. Listen to him, and you shall one day rejoin the spirit whom you must now leave behind. She has been accepted, and will be here always, as young and as happy as she was when I first called her from the land of snows."

When the voice had ceased, the young man awoke. It had been only a dream, and he was still in the bitter land of snows, and hunger, and tears.

Orpheus

The story of a journey to the other world to bring back a loved one is common across North America. It is called the Orpheus theme, after a similar Greek myth.

Orpheus was the greatest of all musicians. He played so wonderfully that animals and birds gathered round to listen, and even the stones and mountains struggled to awaken from their blocky sleep. Orpheus loved the nymph, Eurydice, and they were married. But they had only been married a few days when a snake bit her, and her soul went down to the land of the dead.

Wild with grief, Orpheus went to the underworld to win back his beloved Eurydice. His music so moved Persephone that she convinced Hades to let Eurydice follow Orpheus back to the world of light. There was one condition: Orpheus must go on faith, and not look to see if Eurydice was really following him. If he did, she would have to stay in the underworld for good. The two were almost at the upper world when Orpheus, wracked by uncertainty, could not resist a brief glance behind him: only to see Eurydice fall back, lost forever.

ACKNOWLEDGEMENTS

The publishers have made every effort to trace the source of materials appearing in this book. Information that will enable the publishers to rectify any error or omission will be welcomed.

The Woman Who Fell from the Sky and **How Four Visited Glooscap** from *Indian Legends of Canada*, edited by Ella Elizabeth Clark. Used by permission of the Canadian Publishers, McClelland and Stewart, Toronto.

Yhi Brings the Earth to Life from *Legends of Earth, Air, Fire and Water* by Eric and Tessa Hadley (Cambridge University Press, 1985). Reprinted with the permission of Cambridge University Press and the authors.

The Making of Gods and People from *The God Beneath the Sea* by Leon Garfield and Edward Blishen (Kestrel Books/An imprint of Penguin Books, 1970), reprinted by permission of John Johnson (Authors' Agent) Limited.

The Raven Steals the Light and **How the Raven Lost His Beak** from *The Raven Steals the Light* by Bill Reid and Robert Bringhurst (Douglas & McIntyre, 1984), reprinted by permission of the publisher.

The Archer and the Moon Goddess from *The Magic Pears* by Shiu L. Kong and Elizabeth K. Wong © 1986. Published by Kensington Educational, 52 Granby Street, Toronto, Ontario, M5B 2J5. Reprinted by permission of the authors.

Sedna, Mother of the Sea Animals from *The Day Tuk Became a Hunter*, by Ronald Melzack. Used by permission of the Canadian Publishers, McClelland and Stewart, Toronto.

How the Rivers First Came on Earth and **Anansi Gives Nyame a Child** from *A Treasury of African Folklore*, by Harold Courlander, Crown Publishers, 1975. Copyright 1975 by Harold Courlander. "How the Rivers First Came on Earth" comes originally from *In the Shadow of the Bush*, by P. Amaury Talbot, London, 1912.

Nanabush Creates the World from *The Adventures of Nanabush*, by Emerson and David Coatsworth. Copyright © 1979 by Emerson and David Coatsworth. Published by Doubleday Canada Ltd. Reprinted by permission of Doubleday Canada Ltd.

Coyote and the Fish Dam and **Demeter and Persephone** copyright © Celia Barker Lottridge, 1990.

The Apples of Iduna and **The Death of Balder** from *Thunder of the Gods* by Dorothy Hosford (Henry Holt & Co., 1952).

Hermes, Lord of Robbers from *Hermes, Lord of Robbers*, translated and adapted by Penelope Proddow (Doubleday & Company Inc., n.d.). Translation Copyright © 1971 by Mary Parkinson Proddow.

Beowulf and the Fight with Grendel from *Beowulf* by Rosemary Sutcliff (The Bodley Head, 1961). Reprinted by permission of The Bodley Head.